Hillbilly Elegy

Hillbilly Elegy

A Memoir of a Family
and Culture in Crisis

J.D. VANCE

HARPER

An Imprint of HarperCollins*Publishers*

HarperCollins books may be purchased for educational, business, or sales pro-motional use. For information, please e-mail the Special Markets Department at SPsales@harpercollins.com.

FIRST EDITION

Designed by Leah Carlson-Stanisic

Library of Congress Cataloging-in-Publication Data has been applied for.

ISBN: 978-0-06-230054-6

17   18   19   20   OV/RRD   30 29

For Mamaw and Papaw, my very own hillbilly terminators

Hillbilly Elegy

Introduction

My name is J.D. Vance, and I think I should start with a confession: I find the existence of the book you hold in your hands somewhat absurd. It says right there on the cover that it's a memoir, but I'm thirty-one years old, and I'll be the first to admit that I've accomplished nothing great in my life, certainly nothing that would justify a complete stranger paying money to read about it. The coolest thing I've done, at least on paper, is graduate from Yale Law School, something thirteen-year-old J.D. Vance would have considered ludicrous. But about two hundred people do the same thing every year, and trust me, you don't want to read about most of their lives. I am not a senator, a governor, or a former cabinet secretary. I haven't started a billion-dollar company or a world-changing nonprofit. I have a nice job, a happy marriage, a comfortable home, and two lively dogs.

So I didn't write this book because I've accomplished something extraordinary. I wrote this book because I've achieved something quite ordinary, which doesn't happen to most kids who grow up like me. You see, I grew up poor, in the Rust Belt, in an Ohio steel town that has been hemorrhaging jobs and hope for as long as I can remember. I have, to put it mildly, a complex relationship with my parents, one of whom has struggled with addiction for nearly my entire life. My grandparents, neither of whom graduated from high school, raised me, and few members of even my extended family attended college. The statistics tell you that kids like me face a grim future—that if they're lucky, they'll manage to avoid welfare; and if they're unlucky, they'll die of a heroin overdose, as happened to dozens in my small hometown just last year.

I was one of those kids with a grim future. I almost failed out of high school. I nearly gave in to the deep anger and resentment harbored by everyone around me. Today people look at me, at my job and my Ivy League credentials, and assume that I'm some sort of genius, that only a truly extraordinary person could have made it to where I am today. With all due respect to those people, I think that theory is a load of bullshit. Whatever talents I have, I almost squandered until a handful of loving people rescued me.

That is the real story of my life, and that is why I wrote this book. I want people to know what it feels like to nearly give up on yourself and why you might do it. I want people to understand what happens in the lives of the poor and the psychological impact that spiritual and material poverty has on their children. I want people to understand the American Dream as my family and I encountered it. I want people to understand how upward mobility really feels. And I want people to understand something I learned only recently: that for those of us lucky enough to live the American Dream, the demons of the life we left behind continue to chase us.

There is an ethnic component lurking in the background of my story. In our race-conscious society, our vocabulary often extends no further than the color of someone's skin—"black people," "Asians," "white privilege." Sometimes these broad categories are useful, but to understand my story, you have to delve into the details. I may be white, but I do not identify with the WASPs of the Northeast. Instead, I identify with the millions of working-class white Americans of Scots-Irish descent who have no college degree. To these folks, poverty is the family tradition—their ancestors were day laborers in the Southern slave economy, sharecroppers after that, coal miners after that, and machinists and millworkers during more recent times. Americans call them hillbillies, rednecks, or white trash. I call them neighbors, friends, and family.

The Scots-Irish are one of the most distinctive subgroups in America. As one observer noted, "In traveling across America, the Scots-Irish have consistently blown my mind as far and away the most persistent and unchanging regional subculture in the country. Their family structures, religion and politics, and social lives all remain unchanged compared to the wholesale abandonment of tradition that's occurred nearly everywhere else."[1] This distinctive embrace of cultural tradition comes along with many good traits—an intense sense of loyalty, a fierce dedication to family and country—but also many bad ones. We do not like outsiders or people who are different from us, whether the difference lies in how they look, how they act, or, most important, how they talk. To understand me, you must understand that I am a Scots-Irish hillbilly at heart.

If ethnicity is one side of the coin, then geography is the other. When the first wave of Scots-Irish immigrants landed in the New World in the eighteenth century, they were deeply attracted to

the Appalachian Mountains. This region is admittedly huge—
stretching from Alabama to Georgia in the South to Ohio to
parts of New York in the North—but the culture of Greater
Appalachia is remarkably cohesive. My family, from the hills of
eastern Kentucky, describe themselves as hillbillies, but Hank
Williams, Jr.—born in Louisiana and an Alabama resident—also
identified himself as one in his rural white anthem "A Country
Boy Can Survive." It was Greater Appalachia's political reorien-
tation from Democrat to Republican that redefined American
politics after Nixon. And it is in Greater Appalachia where the
fortunes of working-class whites seem dimmest. From low social
mobility to poverty to divorce and drug addiction, my home is
a hub of misery.

It is unsurprising, then, that we're a pessimistic bunch. What
is more surprising is that, as surveys have found, working-class
whites are the most pessimistic group in America. More pessimistic than Latino immigrants, many of whom suffer unthinkable
poverty. More pessimistic than black Americans, whose material
prospects continue to lag behind those of whites. While reality
permits some degree of cynicism, the fact that hillbillies like me
are more down about the future than many other groups—some
of whom are clearly more destitute than we are—suggests that
something else is going on.

Indeed it is. We're more socially isolated than ever, and we pass
that isolation down to our children. Our religion has changed—
built around churches heavy on emotional rhetoric but light on
the kind of social support necessary to enable poor kids to do
well. Many of us have dropped out of the labor force or have
chosen not to relocate for better opportunities. Our men suffer
from a peculiar crisis of masculinity in which some of the very

traits that our culture inculcates make it difficult to succeed in a changing world.

When I mention the plight of my community, I am often met with an explanation that goes something like this: "Of course the prospects for working-class whites have worsened, J.D., but you're putting the chicken before the egg. They're divorcing more, marrying less, and experiencing less happiness because their economic opportunities have declined. If they only had better access to jobs, other parts of their lives would improve as well."

I once held this opinion myself, and I very desperately wanted to believe it during my youth. It makes sense. Not having a job is stressful, and not having enough money to live on is even more so. As the manufacturing center of the industrial Midwest has hollowed out, the white working class has lost both its economic security and the stable home and family life that comes with it.

But experience can be a difficult teacher, and it taught me that this story of economic insecurity is, at best, incomplete. A few years ago, during the summer before I enrolled at Yale Law School, I was looking for full-time work in order to finance my move to New Haven, Connecticut. A family friend suggested that I work for him in a medium-sized floor tile distribution business near my hometown. Floor tile is extraordinarily heavy: Each piece weighs anywhere from three to six pounds, and it's usually packaged in cartons of eight to twelve pieces. My primary duty was to lift the floor tile onto a shipping pallet and prepare that pallet for departure. It wasn't easy, but it paid thirteen dollars an hour and I needed the money, so I took the job and collected as many overtime shifts and extra hours as I could.

The tile business employed about a dozen people, and most employees had worked there for many years. One guy worked two full-time jobs, but not because he had to: His second job at the tile business allowed him to pursue his dream of piloting an airplane. Thirteen dollars an hour was good money for a single guy in our hometown—a decent apartment costs about five hundred dollars a month—and the tile business offered steady raises. Every employee who worked there for a few years earned at least sixteen dollars an hour in a down economy, which provided an annual income of thirty-two thousand—well above the poverty line even for a family. Despite this relatively stable situation, the managers found it impossible to fill my warehouse position with a long-term employee. By the time I left, three guys worked in the warehouse; at twenty-six, I was by far the oldest.

One guy, I'll call him Bob, joined the tile warehouse just a few months before I did. Bob was nineteen with a pregnant girlfriend. The manager kindly offered the girlfriend a clerical position answering phones. Both of them were terrible workers. The girlfriend missed about every third day of work and never gave advance notice. Though warned to change her habits repeatedly, the girlfriend lasted no more than a few months. Bob missed work about once a week, and he was chronically late. On top of that, he often took three or four daily bathroom breaks, each over half an hour. It became so bad that, by the end of my tenure, another employee and I made a game of it: We'd set a timer when he went to the bathroom and shout the major milestones through the warehouse—"Thirty-five minutes!" "Forty-five minutes!" "One hour!"

Eventually, Bob, too, was fired. When it happened, he lashed out at his manager: "How could you do this to me? Don't you know I've got a pregnant girlfriend?" And he was not alone: At least two other people, including Bob's cousin, lost their jobs or quit during my short time at the tile warehouse.

You can't ignore stories like this when you talk about equal opportunity. Nobel-winning economists worry about the decline of the industrial Midwest and the hollowing out of the economic core of working whites. What they mean is that manufacturing jobs have gone overseas and middle-class jobs are harder to come by for people without college degrees. Fair enough—I worry about those things, too. But this book is about something else: what goes on in the lives of real people when the industrial economy goes south. It's about reacting to bad circumstances in the worst way possible. It's about a culture that increasingly encourages social decay instead of counteracting it.

The problems that I saw at the tile warehouse run far deeper than macroeconomic trends and policy. Too many young men immune to hard work. Good jobs impossible to fill for any length of time. And a young man with every reason to work—a wife-to-be to support and a baby on the way—carelessly tossing aside a good job with excellent health insurance. More troublingly, when it was all over, he thought something had been done *to him*. There is a lack of agency here—a feeling that you have little control over your life and a willingness to blame everyone but yourself. This is distinct from the larger economic landscape of modern America.

It's worth noting that although I focus on the group of people I know—working-class whites with ties to Appalachia—I'm not arguing that we deserve more sympathy than other folks. This is not a story about why white people have more to complain about than black people or any other group. That said, I do hope that readers of this book will be able to take from it an appreciation of how class and family affect the poor without filtering their views through a racial prism. To many analysts, terms like "welfare queen" conjure unfair images of the lazy black mom living on the dole. Readers of this book will realize quickly that there is little relationship between that specter and my argument: I have known many welfare queens; some were my neighbors, and all were white.

This book is not an academic study. In the past few years, William Julius Wilson, Charles Murray, Robert Putnam, and Raj Chetty have authored compelling, well-researched tracts demonstrating that upward mobility fell off in the 1970s and never really recovered, that some regions have fared much worse than others (shocker: Appalachia and the Rust Belt score poorly), and that many of the phenomena I saw in my own life exist across society. I may quibble with some of their conclusions, but they have demonstrated convincingly that America has a problem. Though I will use data, and though I do sometimes rely on academic studies to make a point, my primary aim is not to convince you of a documented problem. My primary aim is to tell a true story about what that problem feels like when you were born with it hanging around your neck.

I cannot tell that story without appealing to the cast of characters who made up my life. So this book is not just a personal memoir but a family one—a history of opportunity and upward mobility viewed through the eyes of a group of hillbillies from Appalachia. Two generations ago, my grandparents were dirt-poor and in love. They got married and moved north in the hope of escaping the dreadful poverty around them. Their grandchild (me) graduated from one of the finest educational institutions in the world. That's the short version. The long version exists in the pages that follow.

Though I sometimes change the names of people to protect their privacy, this story is, to the best of my recollection, a fully accurate portrait of the world I've witnessed. There are no composite characters and no narrative shortcuts. Where possible, I corroborated the details with documentation—report cards, handwritten letters, notes on photographs—but I am sure this story is as fallible as any human memory. Indeed, when I asked my sister to read an earlier draft, that draft ignited a thirty-minute conversation about whether I had misplaced an event chronologically. I left my version in, not because I suspect my sister's memory is faulty (in fact, I imagine hers is better than mine), but because I think there is something to learn in how I've organized the events in my own mind.

Nor am I an unbiased observer. Nearly every person you will read about is deeply flawed. Some have tried to murder other people, and a few were successful. Some have abused their children, physically or emotionally. Many abused (and still abuse) drugs. But I love these people, even those to whom I avoid speaking for my own sanity. And if I leave you with the impression that there are bad people in my life, then I am sorry, both to you and to the people so portrayed. For there are no villains in this story. There's just a ragtag band of hillbillies struggling to find their way—both for their sake and, by the grace of God, for mine.

Chapter 1

————

Like most small children, I learned my home address so that if I got lost, I could tell a grown-up where to take me. In kindergarten, when the teacher asked me where I lived, I could recite the address without skipping a beat, even though my mother changed addresses frequently, for reasons I never understood as a child. Still, I always distinguished "my address" from "my home." My address was where I spent most of my time with my mother and sister, wherever that might be. But my home never changed: my great-grandmother's house, in the holler, in Jackson, Kentucky.

Jackson is a small town of about six thousand in the heart of southeastern Kentucky's coal country. Calling it a town is a bit charitable: There's a courthouse, a few restaurants—almost all of them fast-food chains—and a few other shops and stores. Most of the people live in the mountains surrounding Kentucky Highway 15, in trailer parks, in government-subsidized housing, in small farmhouses, and in mountain homesteads like the one that served as the backdrop for the fondest memories of my childhood.

Jacksonians say hello to everyone, willingly skip their favorite pastimes to dig a stranger's car out of the snow, and—without exception—stop their cars, get out, and stand at attention every time a funeral motorcade drives past. It was that latter practice that made me aware of something special about Jackson and its people. Why, I'd ask my grandma—whom we all called Mamaw—did everyone stop for the passing hearse? "Because, honey, we're hill people. And we respect our dead."

My grandparents left Jackson in the late 1940s and raised their family in Middletown, Ohio, where I later grew up. But until I was twelve, I spent my summers and much of the rest of my time back in Jackson. I'd visit along with Mamaw, who wanted to see friends and family, ever conscious that time was shortening the list of her favorite people. And as time wore on, we made our trips for one reason above all: to take care of Mamaw's mother, whom we called Mamaw Blanton (to distinguish her, though somewhat confusingly, from Mamaw). We stayed with Mamaw Blanton in the house where she'd lived since before her husband left to fight the Japanese in the Pacific.

Mamaw Blanton's house was my favorite place in the world, though it was neither large nor luxurious. The house had three bedrooms. In the front were a small porch, a porch swing, and a large yard that stretched into a mountain on one side and to the head of the holler on the other. Though Mamaw Blanton owned some property, most of it was uninhabitable foliage. There wasn't a backyard to speak of, though there was a beautiful mountainside of rock and tree. There was always the holler, and the creek that ran alongside it; those were backyard enough. The kids all slept in a single upstairs room: a squad bay of about a dozen beds where my cousins and I played late into the night until our irritated grandma would frighten us into sleep.

The surrounding mountains were paradise to a child, and I spent much of my time terrorizing the Appalachian fauna: No turtle, snake, frog, fish, or squirrel was safe. I'd run around with my cousins, unaware of the ever-present poverty or Mamaw Blanton's deteriorating health.

At a deep level, Jackson was the one place that belonged to me, my sister, and Mamaw. I loved Ohio, but it was full of painful memories. In Jackson, I was the grandson of the toughest woman anyone knew and the most skilled auto mechanic in town; in Ohio, I was the abandoned son of a man I hardly knew and a woman I wished I didn't. Mom visited Kentucky only for the annual family reunion or the occasional funeral, and when she did, Mamaw made sure she brought none of the drama. In Jackson, there would be no screaming, no fighting, no beating up on my sister, and especially "no men," as Mamaw would say. Mamaw hated Mom's various love interests and allowed none of them in Kentucky.

In Ohio, I had grown especially skillful at navigating various father figures. With Steve, a midlife-crisis sufferer with an earring to prove it, I pretended earrings were cool—so much so that he thought it appropriate to pierce my ear, too. With Chip, an alcoholic police officer who saw my earring as a sign of "girlieness," I had thick skin and loved police cars. With Ken, an odd man who proposed to Mom three days into their relationship, I was a kind brother to his two children. But none of these things were really true. I hated earrings, I hated police cars, and I knew that Ken's children would be out of my life by the next year. In Kentucky, I didn't have to pretend to be someone I wasn't, because the only men in my life—my grandmother's brothers and brothers-in-law—already knew me. Did I want to make them proud? Of course I did, but not because I pretended to like them; I genuinely loved them.

The oldest and meanest of the Blanton men was Uncle Teaberry, nicknamed for his favorite flavor of chewing gum. Uncle Teaberry, like his father, served in the navy during World War II. He died when I was four, so I have only two real memories of him. In the first, I'm running for my life, and Teaberry is close behind with a switchblade, assuring me that he'll feed my right ear to the dogs if he catches me. I leap into Mamaw Blanton's arms, and the terrifying game is over. But I know that I loved him, because my second memory is of throwing such a fit over not being allowed to visit him on his deathbed that my grandma was forced to don a hospital robe and smuggle me in. I remember clinging to her underneath that hospital robe, but I don't remember saying goodbye.

Uncle Pet came next. Uncle Pet was a tall man with a biting wit and a raunchy sense of humor. The most economically successful of the Blanton crew, Uncle Pet left home early and started some timber and construction businesses that made him enough money to race horses in his spare time. He seemed the nicest of the Blanton men, with the smooth charm of a successful businessman. But that charm masked a fierce temper. Once, when a truck driver delivered supplies to one of Uncle Pet's businesses, he told my old hillbilly uncle, "Off-load this now, you son of a bitch." Uncle Pet took the comment literally: "When you say that, you're calling my dear old mother a bitch, so I'd kindly ask you speak more carefully." When the driver—nicknamed Big Red because of his size and hair color—repeated the insult, Uncle Pet did what any rational business owner would do: He pulled the man from his truck, beat him unconscious, and ran an electric saw up and down his body. Big Red nearly bled to death but was rushed to the hospital and survived. Uncle Pet never went to jail, though. Apparently, Big Red was also an Appalachian man, and he refused to speak to the police about the incident or press charges. He knew what it meant to insult a man's mother.

Uncle David may have been the only one of Mamaw's brothers to care little for that honor culture. An old rebel with long, flowing hair and a longer beard, he loved everything but rules, which might explain why, when I found his giant marijuana plant in the backyard of the old homestead, he didn't try to explain it away. Shocked, I asked Uncle David what he planned to do with illegal drugs. So he got some cigarette papers and a lighter and showed me. I was twelve. I knew if Mamaw ever found out, she'd kill him.

I feared this because, according to family lore, Mamaw *had* nearly killed a man. When she was around twelve, Mamaw walked outside to see two men loading the family's cow—a prized possession in a world without running water—into the back of a truck. She ran inside, grabbed a rifle, and fired a few rounds. One of the men collapsed—the result of a shot to the leg—and the other jumped into the truck and squealed away. The would-be thief could barely crawl, so Mamaw approached him, raised the business end of her rifle to the man's head, and prepared to finish the job. Luckily for him, Uncle Pet intervened. Mamaw's first confirmed kill would have to wait for another day.

Even knowing what a pistol-packing lunatic Mamaw was, I find this story hard to believe. I polled members of my family, and about half had never heard the story. The part I believe is that she would have murdered the man if someone hadn't stopped her. She loathed disloyalty, and there was no greater disloyalty than class betrayal. Each time someone stole a bike from our porch (three times, by my count), or broke into her car and took the loose change, or stole a delivery, she'd tell me, like a general giving his troops marching orders, "There is nothing lower than the poor stealing from the poor. It's hard enough as it is. We sure as hell don't need to make it even harder on each other."

Youngest of all the Blanton boys was Uncle Gary. He was the baby of the family and one of the sweetest men I knew. Uncle Gary left home young and built a successful roofing business in Indiana. A good husband and a better father, he'd always say to me, "We're proud of you, ole Jaydot," causing me to swell with pride. He was my favorite, the only Blanton brother not to threaten me with a kick in the ass or a detached ear.

My grandma also had two younger sisters, Betty and Rose, whom I loved each very much, but I was obsessed with the Blanton men. I would sit among them and beg them to tell and retell their stories. These men were the gatekeepers to the family's oral tradition, and I was their best student.

Most of this tradition was far from child appropriate. Almost all of it involved the kind of violence that should land someone in jail. Much of it centered on how the county in which Jackson was situated—Breathitt—earned its alliterative nickname, "Bloody Breathitt." There were many explanations, but they all had one theme: The people of Breathitt hated certain things, and they didn't need the law to snuff them out.

One of the most common tales of Breathitt's gore revolved around an older man in town who was accused of raping a young girl. Mamaw told me that, days before his trial, the man was found facedown in a local lake with sixteen bullet wounds in his back. The authorities never investigated the murder, and the only mention of the incident appeared in the local newspaper on the morning his body was discovered. In an admirable display of journalistic pith, the paper reported: "Man found dead. Foul play expected." "Foul play expected?" my grandmother would roar. "You're goddamned right. Bloody Breathitt got to that son of a bitch."

Or there was that day when Uncle Teaberry overheard a young man state a desire to "eat her panties," a reference to his sister's (my Mamaw's) undergarments. Uncle Teaberry drove home, retrieved a pair of Mamaw's underwear, and forced the young man—at knifepoint—to consume the clothing.

Some people may conclude that I come from a clan of lunatics. But the stories made me feel like hillbilly royalty, because these were classic good-versus-evil stories, and my people were on the right side. My people were extreme, but extreme in the service of something—defending a sister's honor or ensuring that a criminal paid for his crimes. The Blanton men, like the tomboy Blanton sister whom I called Mamaw, were enforcers of hillbilly justice, and to me, that was the very best kind.

Despite their virtues, or perhaps because of them, the Blanton men were full of vice. A few of them left a trail of neglected children, cheated wives, or both. And I didn't even know them that well: I saw them only at large family reunions or during the holidays. Still, I loved and worshipped them. I once overheard Mamaw tell her mother that I loved the Blanton men because so many father figures had come and gone, but the Blanton men were always there. There's definitely a kernel of truth to that. But more than anything, the Blanton men were the living embodiment of the hills of Kentucky. I loved them because I loved Jackson.

As I grew older, my obsession with the Blanton men faded into appreciation, just as my view of Jackson as some sort of paradise matured. I will always think of Jackson as my home. It is unfathomably beautiful: When the leaves turn in October, it seems as if every mountain in town is on fire. But for all its beauty, and for all the fond memories, Jackson is a very harsh place. Jackson taught me that "hill people" and "poor people" usually meant the same thing. At Mamaw Blanton's, we'd eat scrambled eggs, ham, fried potatoes, and biscuits for breakfast; fried bologna sandwiches for lunch; and soup beans and corn-bread for dinner. Many Jackson families couldn't say the same, and I knew this because, as I grew older, I overheard the adults speak about the pitiful children in the neighborhood who were starving and how the town could help them. Mamaw shielded me from the worst of Jackson, but you can keep reality at bay only so long.

On a recent trip to Jackson, I made sure to stop at Mamaw Blanton's old house, now inhabited by my second cousin Rick and his family. We talked about how things had changed. "Drugs have come in," Rick told me. "And nobody's interested in holding down a job." I hoped my beloved holler had escaped the worst, so I asked Rick's boys to take me on a walk. All around I saw the worst signs of Appalachian poverty.

Some of it was as heartbreaking as it was cliché: decrepit shacks rotting away, stray dogs begging for food, and old fur-niture strewn on the lawns. Some of it was far more troubling. While passing a small two-bedroom house, I noticed a fright-ened set of eyes looking at me from behind the curtains of a bed-room window. My curiosity piqued, I looked closer and counted no fewer than eight pairs of eyes, all looking at me from three windows with an unsettling combination of fear and longing. On the front porch was a thin man, no older than thirty-five, apparently the head of the household. Several ferocious, malnourished, chained-up dogs protected the furniture strewn about the barren front yard. When I asked Rick's son what the young father did for a living, he told me the man had no job and was proud of it. But, he added, "they're mean, so we just try to avoid them."

That house might be extreme, but it represents much about the lives of hill people in Jackson. Nearly a third of the town lives in poverty, a figure that includes about half of Jackson's children. And that doesn't count the large majority of Jacksonians who hover around the poverty line. An epidemic of prescription drug addiction has taken root. The public schools are so bad that the state of Kentucky recently seized control. Nevertheless, parents send their children to these schools because they have little extra money, and the high school fails to send its students to college with alarming consistency. The people are physically unhealthy, and without government assistance they lack treatment for the most basic problems. Most important, they're *mean* about it— they will hesitate to open their lives up to others for the simple reason that they don't wish to be judged.

In 2009, ABC News ran a news report about Appalachian America, highlighting a phenomenon known locally as "Mountain Dew mouth": painful dental problems in young children, generally caused by too much sugary soda. In its broadcast, ABC featured a litany of stories about Appalachian children confronting poverty and deprivation. The news report was widely watched in the region but met with utter scorn. The consistent reaction: This is none of your damn business. "This has to be the most offensive thing I have ever heard and you should all be ashamed, ABC included," wrote one commenter online. Another added: "You should be ashamed of yourself for reinforcing old, false stereotypes and not giving a more accurate picture of Appalachia. This is an opinion shared among many in the actual rural towns of the mountains that I have met."

I knew this because my cousin took to Facebook to silence the critics—noting that only by admitting the region's problems could people hope to change them. Amber is uniquely positioned to comment on the problems of Appalachia: Unlike me, she spent her entire childhood in Jackson. She was an academic star in high school and later earned a college degree, the first in her nuclear family to do so. She saw the worst of Jackson's poverty firsthand and overcame it.

The angry reaction supports the academic literature on Appalachian Americans. In a December 2000 paper, sociologists Carol A. Markstrom, Sheila K. Marshall, and Robin J. Tryon found that avoidance and wishful-thinking forms of coping "significantly predicted resiliency" among Appalachian teens. Their paper suggests that hillbillies learn from an early age to deal with uncomfortable truths by avoiding them, or by pretending better truths exist. This tendency might make for psychological resilience, but it also makes it hard for Appalachians to look at themselves honestly.

We tend to overstate and to understate, to glorify the good and ignore the bad in ourselves. This is why the folks of Appalachia reacted strongly to an honest look at some of its most impoverished people. It's why I worshipped the Blanton men, and it's why I spent the first eighteen years of my life pretending that everything in the world was a problem except me.

The truth is hard, and the hardest truths for hill people are the ones they must tell about themselves. Jackson is undoubtedly full of the nicest people in the world; it is also full of drug addicts and at least one man who can find the time to make eight children but can't find the time to support them. It is unquestionably beautiful, but its beauty is obscured by the environmental waste and loose trash that scatters the countryside. Its people are hardworking, except of course for the many food stamp recipients who show little interest in honest work. Jackson, like the Blanton men, is full of contradictions.

Things have gotten so bad that last summer, after my cousin Mike buried his mother, his thoughts turned immediately to selling her house. "I can't live here, and I can't leave it untended," he said. "The drug addicts will ransack it." Jackson has always been poor, but it was never a place where a man feared leaving his mother's home alone. The place I call home has taken a worrisome turn.

If there is any temptation to judge these problems as the narrow concern of backwoods hollers, a glimpse at my own life reveals that Jackson's plight has gone mainstream. Thanks to the massive migration from the poorer regions of Appalachia to places like Ohio, Michigan, Indiana, Pennsylvania, and Illinois, hillbilly values spread widely along with hillbilly people. Indeed, Kentucky transplants and their children are so prominent in Middletown, Ohio (where I grew up), that as kids we derisively called it "Middletucky."

My grandparents uprooted themselves from the real Kentucky and relocated to Middletucky in search of a better life, and in some ways they found it. In other ways, they never really escaped. The drug addiction that plagues Jackson has afflicted their older daughter for her entire adult life. Mountain Dew mouth may be especially bad in Jackson, but my grandparents fought it in Middletown, too: I was nine months old the first time Mamaw saw my mother put Pepsi in my bottle. Virtuous fathers are in short supply in Jackson, but they are equally scarce in the lives of my grandparents' grandchildren. People have struggled to get out of Jackson for decades; now they struggle to escape Middletown.

If the problems start in Jackson, it is not entirely clear where they end. What I realized many years ago, watching that funeral procession with Mamaw, is that I am a hill person. So is much of America's white working class. And we hill people aren't doing very well.

Chapter 2

Hillbillies like to add their own twist to many words. We call minnows "minners" and crayfish "crawdads." "Hollow" is defined as a "valley or basin," but I've never said the word "hollow" unless I've had to explain to a friend what I mean when I say "holler." Other people have all kinds of names for their grandparents: grandpa, nanna, pop-pop, grannie, and so on. Yet I've never heard anyone say "Mamaw"—pronounced ma'am-aw—or "Papaw" outside of our community. These names belong only to hillbilly grandparents.

My grandparents—Mamaw and Papaw—were, without question or qualification, the best things that ever happened to me. They spent the last two decades of their lives showing me the value of love and stability and teaching me the life lessons that most people learn from their parents. Both did their part to ensure that I had the self-confidence and the right opportunities to get a fair shot at the American Dream. But I doubt that, as children, Jim Vance and Bonnie Blanton ever expected much out of their own lives. How could they? Appalachian hills and single-room, K–12 schoolhouses don't tend to foster big dreams.

We don't know much about Papaw's early years, and I doubt that will ever change. We do know that he was something of hillbilly royalty. Papaw's distant cousin—also Jim Vance—married into the Hatfield family and joined a group of former Confederate soldiers and sympathizers called the Wildcats. When Cousin Jim murdered former Union soldier Asa Harmon McCoy, he kicked off one of the most famous family feuds in American history.

Papaw was born James Lee Vance in 1929, his middle name a tribute to his father, Lee Vance. Lee died just a few months after Papaw's birth, so Papaw's overwhelmed mother, Goldie, sent him to live with her father, Pap Taulbee, a strict man with a small timber business. Though Goldie sent money occasionally, she rarely visited her young son. Papaw would live with Taulbee in Jackson, Kentucky, for the first seventeen years of his life.

Pap Taulbee had a tiny two-room house just a few hundred yards from the Blantons—Blaine and Hattie and their eight children. Hattie felt sorry for the young motherless boy and became a surrogate mother to my grandfather. Jim soon became an extra member of the family: He spent most of his free time running around with the Blanton boys, and he ate most of his meals in Hattie's kitchen. It was only natural that he'd eventually marry her oldest daughter.

Jim married into a rowdy crew. The Blantons were a famous group in Breathitt, and they had a feuding history nearly as illustrious as Papaw's. Mamaw's great-grandfather had been elected county judge at the beginning of the twentieth century, but only after her grandfather, Tilden (the son of the judge), killed a member of a rival family on Election Day.[2] In a *New York Times* story about the violent feud, two things leap out. The first is that Tilden never went to jail for the crime.[3] The second is that, as the *Times* reported, "complications [were] expected." I would imagine so.

When I first read this gruesome story in one of the country's most circulated newspapers, I felt one emotion above all the rest: pride. It's unlikely that any other ancestor of mine has ever appeared in *The New York Times*. Even if they had, I doubt that any deed would make me as proud as a successful feud. And one that could have swung an election, no less! As Mamaw used to say, you can take the boy out of Kentucky, but you can't take Kentucky out of the boy.

I can't imagine what Papaw was thinking. Mamaw came from a family that would shoot at you rather than argue with you. Her father was a scary old hillbilly with the mouth and war medals of a sailor. Her grandfather's murderous exploits were impressive enough to make the pages of *The New York Times*. And as scary as her lineage was, Mamaw Bonnie herself was so terrifying that, many decades later, a Marine Corps recruiter would tell me that I'd find boot camp easier than living at home. "Those drill instructors are mean," he said. "But not like that grandma of yours." That meanness wasn't enough to dissuade my grandfather. So Mamaw and Papaw were married as teenagers in Jackson, in 1947.

At that time, as the post–World War II euphoria wore off and people began to adjust to a world at peace, there were two types of people in Jackson: those who uprooted their lives and planted them in the industrial powerhouses of the new America, and those who didn't. At the tender ages of fourteen and seventeen, my grandparents had to decide which group to join.

As Papaw once told me, the sole option for many of his friends was to work "in the mines"—mining coal not far from Jackson.

Those who stayed in Jackson spent their lives on the edge of poverty, if not submerged in it. So, soon after marrying, Papaw uprooted his young family and moved to Middletown, a small Ohio town with a rapidly growing industrialized economy.

This is the story my grandparents told me, and like most family legends it's largely true but plays fast and loose with the details. On a recent trip to visit family in Jackson, my great-uncle Arch—Mamaw's brother-in-law and the last of that generation of Jacksonians—introduced me to Bonnie South, a woman who'd spent all of her eighty-four years a hundred yards from Mamaw's childhood home. Until Mamaw left for Ohio, Bonnie South was her best friend. And by Bonnie South's reckoning, Mamaw and Papaw's departure involved a bit more scandal than any of us realized.

In 1946, Bonnie South and Papaw were lovers. I'm not sure what this meant in Jackson at the time—whether they were preparing for an engagement or just passing the time together. Bonnie had little to say of Papaw besides the fact that he was "very handsome." The only other thing Bonnie South recalled was that, at some point in 1946, Papaw cheated on Bonnie with her best friend—Mamaw. Mamaw was thirteen and Papaw sixteen, but the affair produced a pregnancy. And that pregnancy added a number of pressures that made *right now* the time to leave Jackson: my intimidating, grizzled war-veteran great-grandfather; the Blanton Brothers, who had already earned a reputation for defending Mamaw's honor; and an interconnected group of gun-toting hillbillies who immediately knew all about Bonnie Blanton's pregnancy. Most important, Bonnie and Jim Vance would soon have another mouth to feed before they'd gotten used to feeding themselves. Mamaw and Papaw left abruptly for Dayton,

Ohio, where they lived briefly before settling permanently in Middletown.

In later years, Mamaw sometimes spoke of a daughter who died in infancy, and she led us all to believe that the daughter was born sometime after Uncle Jimmy, Mamaw and Papaw's eldest child. Mamaw suffered eight miscarriages in the decade between Uncle Jimmy's birth and my mother's. But recently my sister discovered a birth certificate for "Infant" Vance, the aunt I never knew, who died so young that her birth certificate also lists her date of death. The baby who brought my grandparents to Ohio didn't survive her first week. On that birth certificate, the baby's brokenhearted mother lied about her age: Only fourteen at the time and with a seventeen-year-old husband, she couldn't tell the truth, lest they ship her back to Jackson or send Papaw to jail.

Mamaw's first foray into adulthood ended in tragedy. Today I often wonder: Without the baby, would she ever have left Jackson? Would she have run off with Jim Vance to foreign territory? Mamaw's entire life—and the trajectory of our family—may have changed for a baby who lived only six days.

Whatever mix of economic opportunity and family necessity catapulted my grandparents to Ohio, they were there, and there was no going back. So Papaw found a job at Armco, a large steel company that aggressively recruited in eastern Kentucky coal country. Armco representatives would descend on towns like Jackson and promise (truthfully) a better life for those willing to move north and work in the mills. A special policy encouraged wholesale migration: Applicants with a family member working at Armco would move to the top of the employment list. Armco didn't just hire the young men of Appalachian Kentucky; they actively encouraged those men to bring their extended families.

A number of industrial firms employed a similar strategy, and it appears to have worked. During that era, there were many Jacksons and many Middletowns. Researchers have documented two major waves of migration from Appalachia to the industrial powerhouse economies in the Midwest. The first happened after World War I, when returning veterans found it nearly impossible to find work in the not-yet-industrialized mountains of Kentucky, West Virginia, and Tennessee. It ended as the Great Depression hit Northern economies hard.[4] My grandparents were part of the second wave, composed of returning veterans and the rapidly rising number of young adults in 1940s and '50s Appalachia.[5] As the economies of Kentucky and West Virginia lagged behind those of their neighbors, the mountains had only two products that the industrial economies of the North needed: coal and hill people. And Appalachia exported a lot of both.

Precise numbers are tough to pin down because studies typically measure "net out-migration"—as in the total number of people who left minus the number of people who came in. Many families constantly traveled back and forth, which skews the data. But it is certain that many millions of people traveled along the "hillbilly highway"—a metaphorical term that captured the opinion of Northerners who saw their cities and towns flooded with people like my grandparents. The scale of the migration was staggering. In the 1950s, thirteen of every one hundred Kentucky residents migrated out of the state. Some areas saw even greater emigration: Harlan County, for example, which was brought to fame in an Academy Award–winning documentary about coal strikes, lost 30 percent of its population to migration. In 1960, of Ohio's ten million residents, one million were born in Kentucky, West Virginia, or Tennessee. This doesn't count the

large number of migrants from elsewhere in the southern Appalachian Mountains; nor does it include the children or grandchildren of migrants who were hill people to the core. There were
undoubtedly many of these children and grandchildren, as hillbillies tended to have much higher birthrates than the native
population.[6]

In short, my grandparents' experience was extremely common.
Significant parts of an entire region picked up shop and moved
north. Need more proof? Hop on a northbound highway in Kentucky or Tennessee the day after Thanksgiving or Christmas, and
virtually every license plate you see comes from Ohio, Indiana,
or Michigan—cars full of hillbilly transplants returning home
for the holidays.

Mamaw's family participated in the migratory flow with
gusto. Of her seven siblings, Pet, Paul, and Gary moved to Indiana and worked in construction. Each owned a successful business and earned considerable wealth in the process. Rose, Betty,
Teaberry, and David stayed behind. All of them struggled financially, though everyone but David managed a life of relative
comfort by the standards of their community. The four who left
died on a significantly higher rung of the socioeconomic ladder
than the four who stayed. As Papaw knew when he was a young
man, the best way up for the hillbilly was out.

It was probably uncommon for my grandparents to be alone in
their new city. But if Mamaw and Papaw were isolated from their
family, they were hardly segregated from Middletown's broader
population. Most of the city's inhabitants had moved there for
work in the new industrial plants, and most of these new workers
were from Appalachia. The family-based hiring practices of the
major industrial firms[7] had their desired effect, and the results

were predictable. All over the industrial Midwest, new communities of Appalachian transplants and their families sprang up, virtually out of nowhere. As one study noted, "Migration did not so much destroy neighborhoods and families as transport them."[8] In 1950s Middletown, my grandparents found themselves in a situation both new and familiar. New because they were, for the first time, cut off from the extended Appalachian support network to which they were accustomed; familiar because they were still surrounded by hillbillies.

I'd like to tell you how my grandparents thrived in their new environment, how they raised a successful family, and how they retired comfortably middle-class. But that is a partial truth. The full truth is that my grandparents struggled in their new life, and they continued to do so for decades.

For starters, a remarkable stigma attached to people who left the hills of Kentucky for a better life. Hillbillies have a phrase—"too big for your britches"—to describe those who think they're better than the stock they came from. For a long time after my grandparents came to Ohio, they heard exactly that phrase from people back home. The sense that they had abandoned their families was acute, and it was expected that, whatever their responsibilities, they would return home regularly. This pattern was common among Appalachian migrants: More than nine in ten would make visits "home" during the course of their lives, and more than one in ten visited about once a month.[9] My grandparents returned to Jackson often, sometimes on consecutive weekends, despite the fact that the trip in the 1950s required about twenty hours of driving. Economic mobility came with a lot of pressures, and it came with a lot of new responsibilities.

That stigma came from both directions: Many of their new neighbors viewed them suspiciously. To the established middle class of white Ohioans, these hillbillies simply didn't belong. They had too many children, and they welcomed their extended families into their homes for too long. On several occasions, Mamaw's brothers and sisters lived with her and Papaw for months as they tried to find good work outside of the hills. In other words, many parts of their culture and customs met with roaring disapproval from native Middletonians. As one book, *Appalachian Odyssey*, notes about the influx of hill people to Detroit: "It was not simply that the Appalachian migrants, as rural strangers 'out of place' in the city, were upsetting to Midwestern, urban whites. Rather, these migrants disrupted a broad set of assumptions held by northern whites about how white people appeared, spoke, and behaved . . . the disturbing aspect of *hillbillies* was their racialness. Ostensibly, they were of the same racial order (whites) as those who dominated economic, political, and social power in local and national arenas. But *hillbillies* shared many regional characteristics with the southern blacks arriving in Detroit."[10]

One of Papaw's good friends—a hillbilly from Kentucky whom he met in Ohio—became the mail carrier in their neighborhood. Not long after he moved, the mail carrier got embroiled in a battle with the Middletown government over the flock of chickens that he kept in his yard. He treated them just as Mamaw had treated her chickens back in the holler: Every morning he collected all the eggs, and when his chicken population grew too large, he'd take a few of the old ones, wring their necks, and carve them up for meat right in his backyard. You can just imagine a well-bred housewife watching out the window in horror as her Kentucky-born neighbor slaughtered squawking chickens just a few feet away. My sister and I still call the old mail carrier "the chicken man," and years later even a mention of how the city government ganged up on the chicken man could inspire Mamaw's trademark vitriol: "Fucking zoning laws. They can kiss my ruby-red asshole."

The move to Middletown created other problems, as well. In the mountain homes of Jackson, privacy was more theory than practice. Family, friends, and neighbors would barge into your home without much warning. Mothers would tell their daughters how to raise their children. Fathers would tell sons how to do their jobs. Brothers would tell brothers-in-law how to treat their wives. Family life was something people learned on the fly with a lot of help from their neighbors. In Middletown, a man's home was his castle.

However, that castle was empty for Mamaw and Papaw. They brought an ancient family structure from the hills and tried to make it work in a world of privacy and nuclear families. They were newlyweds, but they didn't have anyone to teach them about marriage. They were parents, but there were no grandparents, aunts, uncles, or cousins to help them with the workload. The only nearby close relative was Papaw's mother, Goldie. She was mostly a stranger to her own son, and Mamaw couldn't have held her in lower esteem for abandoning him.

After a few years, Mamaw and Papaw began to adapt. Mamaw became close friends with the "neighbor lady" (that was her word for the neighbors she liked) who lived in a nearby apartment; Papaw worked on cars in his spare time, and his coworkers slowly turned from colleagues to friends. In 1951 they welcomed a baby boy—my uncle Jimmy—and showered him with their new material comforts. Jimmy, Mamaw would tell me later, could sit up at two weeks, walk at four months, speak in complete sentences just after his first birthday, and read classic novels by age three ("A slight exaggeration," my uncle later admitted). They visited Mamaw's brothers in Indianapolis and picnicked with their new friends. It was, Uncle Jimmy told me, "a typical middle-class life." Kind of boring, by some standards, but happy in a way you appreciate only when you understand the consequences of not being boring.

Which is not to say that things always proceeded smoothly. Once, they traveled to the mall to buy Christmas presents with the holiday throng and let Jimmy roam so he could locate a toy he coveted. "They were advertising it on television," he told me recently. "It was a plastic console that looked like the dash of a jet fighter plane. You could shine a light or shoot darts. The whole idea was to pretend that you were a fighter pilot."

Jimmy wandered into a pharmacy that happened to sell the toy, so he picked it up and began to play with it. "The store clerk wasn't happy. He told me to put the toy down and get out." Chastised, young Jimmy stood outside in the cold until Mamaw and Papaw strolled by and asked if he'd like to go inside the pharmacy.

"I can't," Jimmy told his father.

"Why?"

"I just can't."

"Tell me why right now."

He pointed at the store clerk. "That man got mad at me and told me to leave. I'm not allowed to go back inside."

Mamaw and Papaw stormed in, demanding an explanation for the clerk's rudeness. The clerk explained that Jimmy had been playing with an expensive toy. "This toy?" Papaw asked, picking up the toy. When the clerk nodded, Papaw smashed it on the ground. Utter chaos ensued. As Uncle Jimmy explained, "They went nuts. Dad threw another of the toys across the store and moved toward the clerk in a very menacing way; Mom started grabbing random shit off the shelves and throwing it all over the place. She's screaming, 'Kick his fucking ass! Kick his fucking ass!' And then Dad leans in to this clerk and says very clearly, 'If you say another word to my son, I will break your fucking neck.' This poor guy was completely terrified, and I just wanted to get the hell out of there." The man apologized, and the Vances continued with their Christmas shopping as if nothing had happened.

So, yes, even in their best times, Mamaw and Papaw struggled to adapt. Middletown was a different world. Papaw was supposed to go to work and complain politely to management about rude pharmacy employees. Mamaw was expected to cook dinner, do laundry, and take care of the children. But sewing circles, picnics, and door-to-door vacuum salesmen were not suited to a woman who had almost killed a man at the tender age of twelve. Mamaw had little help when the children were young and required constant supervision, and she had nothing else to do with her time. Decades later she would remember how isolated she felt in the slow suburban crawl of midcentury Middletown. Of that era, she said with characteristic bluntness: "Women were just shit on all the time."

Mamaw had her dreams but never the opportunity to pursue them. Her greatest love was children, in both a specific sense (her children and grandchildren were the only things in the world she seemed to enjoy in old age) and a general one (she watched shows about abused, neglected, and missing kids and used what little spare money she had to purchase shoes and school supplies for the neighborhood's poorest children). She seemed to feel the pain of neglected kids in a deeply personal way and spoke often of how she hated people who mistreated children. I never understood where this sentiment came from—whether she herself was abused as a child, perhaps, or whether she just regretted that her childhood had ended so abruptly. There is a story there, though I'll likely never hear it.

Mamaw dreamed of turning that passion into a career as a children's attorney—serving as a voice for those who lacked one. She never pursued that dream, possibly because she didn't know what becoming an attorney took. Mamaw never spent a day in high school. She'd given birth to and buried a child before she could legally drive a car. Even if she'd known what was required, her new lifestyle offered little encouragement or opportunity for an aspiring law student with three children and a husband.

Despite the setbacks, both of my grandparents had an almost religious faith in hard work and the American Dream. Neither was under any illusions that wealth or privilege didn't matter in America. On politics, for example, Mamaw had one opinion—"They're all a bunch of crooks"—but Papaw became a committed Democrat. He had no problem with Armco, but he and everyone like him hated the coal companies in Kentucky thanks to a long history of labor strife. So, to Papaw and Mamaw, not all rich people were bad, but all bad people were rich. Papaw was a Democrat because that party protected the working people. This attitude carried over to Mamaw: All politicians might be crooks, but if there were any exceptions, they were undoubtedly members of Franklin Delano Roosevelt's New Deal coalition.

Still, Mamaw and Papaw believed that hard work mattered more. They knew that life was a struggle, and though the odds were a bit longer for people like them, that fact didn't excuse failure. "Never be like these fucking losers who think the deck is stacked against them," my grandma often told me. "You can do anything you want to."

Their community shared this faith, and in the 1950s that faith appeared well founded. Within two generations, the transplanted hillbillies had largely caught up to the native population in terms of income and poverty level. Yet their financial success masked their cultural unease, and if my grandparents caught up economically, I wonder if they ever truly assimilated. They always had one foot in the new life and one foot in the old one. They slowly acquired a small number of friends but remained strongly rooted in their Kentucky homeland. They hated domesticated animals and had little use for "critters" that weren't for eating, yet they eventually relented to the children's demands for dogs and cats.

Their children, though, were different. My mom's generation was the first to grow up in the industrial Midwest, far from the deep twangs and one-room schools of the hills. They attended modern high schools with thousands of other students. To my grandparents, the goal was to get out of Kentucky and give their kids a head start. The kids, in turn, were expected to do something with that head start. It didn't quite work out that way.

Before Lyndon Johnson and the Appalachian Regional Commission brought new roads to southeastern Kentucky, the primary road from Jackson to Ohio was U.S. Route 23. So important was this road in the massive hillbilly migration that Dwight Yoakam penned a song about northerners who castigated Appalachian children for learning the wrong three R's: "Reading, Rightin', Rt. 23." Yoakam's song about his own move from southeastern Kentucky could have come from Mamaw's diary:

> *They thought readin', writin', Route 23 would take them to the*
>   *good life that they had never seen;*
> *They didn't know that old highway would lead them to a world*
>   *of misery*

Mamaw and Papaw may have made it out of Kentucky, but they and their children learned the hard way that Route 23 didn't lead where they hoped.

Chapter 3

Mamaw and Papaw had three kids—Jimmy, Bev (my mom), and
Lori. Jimmy was born in 1951, when Mamaw and Papaw were in-
tegrating into their new lives. They wanted more children, so they
tried and tried, through a heartbreaking period of terrible luck
and numerous miscarriages. Mamaw carried the emotional scars
of nine lost children for her entire life. In college I learned that extreme stress can cause miscarriages and that this is especially true
during the early part of a pregnancy. I can't help but wonder how
many additional aunts and uncles I'd have today were it not for my
grandparents' difficult early transition, no doubt intensified by Papaw's years of hard drinking. Yet they persisted through a decade
of failed pregnancies, and eventually it paid off: Mom was born on
January 20, 1961—the day of John F. Kennedy's inauguration—
and my aunt Lori came along less than two years later. For whatever reason, Mamaw and Papaw stopped there.

Uncle Jimmy once told me about the time before his sisters
were born: "We were just a happy, normal middle-class family. I
remember watching *Leave It to Beaver* on TV and thinking that
looked like us." When he first told me this, I nodded attentively

and left it alone. Looking back, I realize, that to most outsiders, a statement like that must come off as insane. Normal middle-class parents don't wreck pharmacies because a store clerk is mildly rude to their child. But that's probably the wrong standard to use. Destroying store merchandise and threatening a sales clerk were normal to Mamaw and Papaw: That's what Scots-Irish Appalachians do when people mess with your kid. "What I mean is that they were united, they were getting along with each other," Uncle Jimmy conceded when I later pressed him. "But yeah, like everyone else in our family, they could go from zero to murderous in a fucking heartbeat."

Whatever unity they possessed early in their marriage began to evaporate after their daughter Lori—whom I call Aunt Wee—was born in 1962. By the mid–1960s, Papaw's drinking had become habitual; Mamaw began to shut herself off from the outside world. Neighborhood kids warned the mailman to avoid the "evil witch" of McKinley Street. When the mailman ignored their advice, he met a large woman with an extra-long menthol cigarette hanging out of her mouth who told him to stay the fuck off of her property. "Hoarder" hadn't entered everyday parlance, but Mamaw fit the bill, and her tendencies only worsened as she withdrew from the world. Garbage piled up in the house, with an entire bedroom devoted to trinkets and debris that had no earthly value.

To hear of this period, one gets the sense that Mamaw and Papaw led two lives. There was the outward public life. It included work during the day and preparing the kids for school. This was the life that everyone else saw, and by all measures it was quite successful: My grandfather earned a wage that was almost unfathomable to friends back home; he liked his work and did it well; their children went to modern, well-funded schools;

and my grandmother lived in a home that was, by Jackson standards, a mansion—two thousand square feet, four bedrooms, and modern plumbing.

Home life was different. "I didn't notice it at first as a teenager," Uncle Jimmy recalled. "At that age, you're just so wrapped up in your own stuff that you hardly recognize the change. But it was there. Dad stayed out more; Mom stopped keeping the house—dirty dishes and junk piled up everywhere. They fought a lot more. It was all around a rough time."

Hillbilly culture at the time (and maybe now) blended a robust sense of honor, devotion to family, and bizarre sexism into a sometimes explosive mix. Before Mamaw was married, her brothers had been willing to murder boys who disrespected their sister. Now that she was married to a man whom many of them considered more a brother than an outsider, they tolerated behavior that would have gotten Papaw killed in the holler. "Mom's brothers would come up and want to go carousing with Dad," Uncle Jimmy explained. "They'd go drinking and chasing women. Uncle Pet was always the leader. I didn't want to hear about it, but I always did. It was that culture from back then that expected the men were going to go out and do what they wanted to do."

Mamaw felt disloyalty acutely. She loathed anything that smacked of a lack of complete devotion to family. In her own home, she'd say things like "I'm sorry I'm so damned mean" and "You know I love you, but I'm just a crazy bitch." But if she knew of anyone criticizing so much as her socks to an outsider, she'd fly off the handle. "I don't know those people. You never talk about family to some stranger. Never." My sister, Lindsay, and I could fight like cats and dogs in her home, and for the most part she'd let us figure things out alone. But if I told a friend that my sister was hateful and Mamaw overheard, she'd remember it and tell me the next time we were alone that I had committed the cardinal sin of disloyalty. "How *dare* you speak about your sister to some little shit? In five years you won't even remember his goddamned name. But your sister is the only true friend you'll ever have." Yet in her own life, with three children at home, the men who should have been most loyal to her—her brothers and husband—conspired against her.

Papaw seemed to resist the social expectations of a middle-class father, sometimes with hilarious results. He would announce that he was headed to the store and ask his kids if they needed anything; he'd come back with a new car. A new Chevrolet convertible one month. A luxurious Oldsmobile the next. "Where'd you get that?" they'd ask him. "It's mine, I traded for it," he'd reply nonchalantly.

But sometimes his failure to conform brought terrible consequences. My young aunt and mother would play a little game when their father came home from work. Some days he would carefully park his car, and the game would go well—their father would come inside, they'd have dinner together like a normal family, and they'd make one another laugh. Many days, however, he wouldn't park his car normally—he'd back into a spot too quickly, or sloppily leave his car on the road, or even sideswipe a telephone pole as he maneuvered. Those days the game was already lost. Mom and Aunt Wee would run inside and tell Mamaw that Papaw had come home drunk. Sometimes they'd run out the back door and stay the night with Mamaw's friends. Other times Mamaw would insist on staying, so Mom and Aunt Wee would brace for a long night. One Christmas Eve, Papaw came home drunk and demanded a fresh dinner. When that failed to materialize, he picked up the family Christmas tree and threw it out the back door. The next year he greeted a crowd at his daughter's birthday party and promptly coughed up a huge wad of phlegm at everyone's feet. Then he smiled and walked off to grab himself another beer.

I couldn't believe that mild-mannered Papaw, whom I adored as a child, was such a violent drunk. His behavior was due at least partly to Mamaw's disposition. She was a violent nondrunk. And she channeled her frustrations into the most productive activity imaginable: covert war. When Papaw passed out on the couch, she'd cut his pants with scissors so they'd burst at the seam when he next sat down. Or she'd steal his wallet and hide it in the oven just to piss him off. When he came home from work and demanded fresh dinner, she'd carefully prepare a plate of fresh garbage. If he was in a fighting mood, she'd fight back. In short, she devoted herself to making his drunken life a living hell.

If Jimmy's youth shielded him from the signs of their deteriorating marriage for a bit, the problem soon reached an obvious nadir. Uncle Jimmy recalled one fight: "I could hear the furniture bumping and bumping, and they were really getting into it. They were both screaming. I went downstairs to beg them to stop." But they didn't stop. Mamaw grabbed a flower vase, hurled it, and—she always had a hell of an arm—hit Papaw right between the eyes. "It split his forehead wide open, and he was bleeding really badly when he got in his car and drove off. That's what I went to school the next day thinking about."

Mamaw told Papaw after a particularly violent night of drinking that if he ever came home drunk again, she'd kill him. A week later, he came home drunk again and fell asleep on the couch. Mamaw, never one to tell a lie, calmly retrieved a gasoline canister from the garage, poured it all over her husband, lit a match, and dropped it on his chest. When Papaw burst into flames, their eleven-year-old daughter jumped into action to put out the fire and save his life. Miraculously, Papaw survived the episode with only mild burns.

Because they were hill people, they had to keep their two lives separate. No outsiders could know about the familial strife—with outsiders defined very broadly. When Jimmy turned eighteen, he took a job at Armco and moved out immediately. Not long after he left, Aunt Wee found herself in the middle of one particularly bad fight, and Papaw punched her in the face. The blow, though accidental, left a nasty black eye. When Jimmy—her own brother—returned home for a visit, Aunt Wee was made to hide in the basement. Because Jimmy didn't live with the family anymore, he was not to know about the inner workings of the house. "That's just how everyone, especially Mamaw, dealt with things," Aunt Wee said. "It was just too embarrassing."

It's not obvious to anyone why Mamaw and Papaw's marriage fell apart. Perhaps Papaw's alcoholism got the best of him. Uncle Jimmy suspects that he eventually "ran around" on Mamaw. Or maybe Mamaw just cracked—with three living kids, one dead one, and a host of miscarriages in between, who could have blamed her?

Despite their violent marriage, Mamaw and Papaw always maintained a measured optimism about their children's futures. They reasoned that if they could go from a one-room schoolhouse in Jackson to a two-story suburban home with the comforts of the middle class, then their children (and grandchildren) should have no problem attending college and acquiring a share of the American Dream. They were unquestionably wealthier than the family members who had stayed in Kentucky. They visited the Atlantic Ocean and Niagara Falls as adults despite never traveling farther than Cincinnati as children. They believed that they had made it and that their children would go even further.

There was something deeply naive about that attitude, though. All three children were profoundly affected by their tumultuous home life. Papaw wanted Jimmy to get an education instead of slogging it out in the steel mill. He warned that if Jimmy got a full-time job out of high school, the money would be like a drug—it would feel good in the short term, but it would keep him from the things he ought to be doing. Papaw even prevented Jimmy from using him as a referral on his Armco application. What Papaw didn't appreciate was that Armco offered something more than money: the ability to get out of a house where your mother threw vases at your father's forehead.

Lori struggled in school, mostly because she never attended class. Mamaw used to joke that she'd drive her to school and drop her off, and somehow Lori would beat her home. During her sophomore year of high school, Lori's boyfriend stole some PCP, and the two of them returned to Mamaw's to indulge. "He told me that he should do more, since he was bigger. That was the last thing I remembered." Lori woke up when Mamaw and her friend Kathy placed Lori in a cold bathtub. Her boyfriend, meanwhile, wasn't responding. Kathy couldn't tell if the young man was breathing. Mamaw ordered her to drag him to the park across the street. "I don't want him to die in my fucking house," she said. Instead she called someone to take him to the hospital, where he spent five days in intensive care.

The next year, at sixteen, Lori dropped out of high school and married. She immediately found herself trapped in an abusive home just like the one she'd tried to escape. Her new husband would lock her in a bedroom to keep her from seeing her family. "It was almost like a prison," Aunt Wee later told me.

Fortunately, both Jimmy and Lori found their way. Jimmy worked his way through night school and landed a sales job with Johnson & Johnson. He was the first person in my family to have a "career." By the time she turned thirty, Lori was working in radiology and had such a nice new husband that Mamaw told the entire family, "If they ever get divorced, I'm following him."

Unfortunately, the statistics caught up with the Vance family, and Bev (my mom) didn't fare so well. Like her siblings, she left home early. She was a promising student, but when she got pregnant at eighteen, she decided college had to wait. After high school, she married her boyfriend and tried to settle down. But settling down wasn't quite her thing: She had learned the lessons of her childhood all too well. When her new life developed the same fighting and drama so present in her old one, Mom filed for divorce and began life as a single mother. She was nineteen, with no degree, no husband, and a little girl—my sister, Lindsay.

Mamaw and Papaw eventually got their act together. Papaw quit drinking in 1983, a decision accompanied by no medical intervention and not much fanfare. He simply stopped and said little about it. He and Mamaw separated and then reconciled, and although they continued to live in separate houses, they spent nearly every waking hour together. And they tried to repair the damage they had wrought: They helped Lori break out of her abusive marriage. They lent money to Bev and helped her with child care. They offered her places to stay, supported her through rehab, and paid for her nursing school. Most important, they filled the gap when my mom was unwilling or unable to be the type of parent that they wished they'd been to her. Mamaw and Papaw may have failed Bev in her youth. But they spent the rest of their lives making up for it.

Chapter 4

————

I was born in late summer 1984, just a few months before Papaw cast his first and only vote for a Republican—Ronald Reagan. Winning large blocks of Rust Belt Democrats like Papaw, Reagan went on to the biggest electoral landslide in modern American history. "I never liked Reagan much," Papaw later told me. "But I hated that son of a bitch Mondale." Reagan's Democratic opponent, a well-educated Northern liberal, stood in stark cultural contrast to my hillbilly Papaw. Mondale never had a chance, and after he departed from the political scene, Papaw never again voted against his beloved "party of the workingman."

Jackson, Kentucky, would always have my heart, but Middletown, Ohio, had most of my time. In many ways, the town where I was born was largely the same as the one my grandparents had migrated to four decades earlier. Its population had changed little since the 1950s, when the flood of migrants on the hillbilly highway slowed to a dribble. My elementary school was built in the 1930s, before my grandparents left Jackson, and my middle school first welcomed a class shortly after World War I, well before my grandparents were born. Armco remained the town's biggest employer, and though troubling signs were on the horizon, Middletown had avoided significant economic problems. "We saw ourselves as a really fine community, on par with Shaker Heights or Upper Arlington," explained a decades-long veteran of the public schools, comparing the Middletown of yore to some of the most successful of Ohio's suburbs. "Of course, none of us knew what would happen."

Middletown is one of the older incorporated towns in Ohio, built during the 1800s thanks to its proximity to the Miami River, which empties directly into the Ohio. As kids, we joked that our hometown was so generic that they didn't even bother to give it a real name: It's in the middle of Cincinnati and Dayton, and it's a town, so here we are. (It's not alone: A few miles from Middletown is Centerville.) Middletown is generic in other ways. It exemplified the economic expansion of the manufacturing-based Rust Belt town. Socioeconomically, it is largely working-class. Racially, there are lots of white and black people (the latter the product of an analogous great migration) but few others. And culturally, it is very conservative, although cultural conservatism and political conservatism are not always aligned in Middletown.

The people I grew up around are not all that dissimilar from the people of Jackson. This is especially obvious at Armco, which employed a plurality of the town's population. Indeed, the work environment once mirrored the Kentucky towns that many of the employees came from. One author reported that "a sign over a doorway between departments read, 'Leave Morgan County and Enter Wolfe County.'"[11] Kentucky—down to its county rivalries—moved with the Appalachian migrants to town.

As a kid, I sorted Middletown into three basic geographic regions. First, the area surrounding the high school, which opened in 1969, Uncle Jimmy's senior year. (Even in 2003, Mamaw called it the "new high school.") The "rich" kids lived here. Large homes mixed comfortably with well-kept parks and office complexes. If your dad was a doctor, he almost certainly owned a home or had an office here, if not both. I dreamed that I'd own a house in Manchester Manor, a relatively new development not a mile from the high school, where a nice home went for less than a fifth of the price of a decent house in San Francisco. Next, the poor kids (the really poor kids) lived near Armco, where even the nice homes had been converted into multi-family apartment units. I didn't know until recently that this neighborhood was actually two neighborhoods—one inhabited by Middletown's working-class black population, the other by its poorest white population. Middletown's few housing projects stood there.

Then there was the area where we lived—mostly single-family homes, with abandoned warehouses and factories within walking distance. Looking back, I don't know if the "really poor" areas and my block were any different, or whether these divisions were the constructs of a mind that didn't want to believe it was *really* poor.

Across the street from our house was Miami Park, a single city block with a swing set, a tennis court, a baseball field, and a basketball court. As I grew up, I noticed that the tennis court lines faded with each passing month, and that the city had stopped filling in the cracks or replacing the nets on the basketball courts. I was still young when the tennis court became little more than a cement block littered with grass patches. I learned that our neighborhood had "gone downhill" after two bikes were stolen in the course of the week. For years, Mamaw said, her children had left their bikes unchained in the yard with no problems. Now her grandkids woke to find thick locks cracked in two by dead-bolt cutters. From that point forward, I walked.

If Middletown had changed little by the time I was born, the writing was on the wall almost immediately thereafter. It's easy even for residents to miss it because the change has been gradual—more erosion than mudslide. But it's obvious if you know where to look, and a common refrain for those of us who return intermittently is "Geez, Middletown is not looking good."

In the 1980s, Middletown had a proud, almost idyllic downtown: a bustling shopping center, restaurants that had operated since before World War II, and a few bars where men like Papaw would gather and have a beer (or many) after a hard day at the steel mill. My favorite store was the local Kmart, which was the main attraction in a strip mall, near a branch of Dillman's—a local grocer with three or four locations. Now the strip mall is mostly bare: Kmart stands empty, and the Dillman family closed that big store and all the rest, too. The last I checked, there was only an Arby's, a discount grocery store, and a Chinese buffet in what was once a Middletown center of commerce. The scene at that strip mall is hardly uncommon. Few Middletown businesses are doing well, and many have ceased operating altogether. Twenty years ago, there were two local malls. Now one of those malls is a parking lot, and the other serves as a walking course for the elderly (though it still has a few stores).

Today downtown Middletown is little more than a relic of American industrial glory. Abandoned shops with broken windows line the heart of downtown, where Central Avenue and Main Street meet. Richie's pawnshop has long since closed, though a hideous yellow and green sign still marks the site, so far as I know. Richie's isn't far from an old pharmacy that, in its heyday, had a soda bar and served root beer floats. Across the street is a building that looks like a theater, with one of those giant triangular signs that reads "ST___L" because the letters in the middle were shattered and never replaced. If you need a payday lender or a cash-for-gold store, downtown Middletown is the place to be.

Not far from the main drag of empty shops and boarded-up windows is the Sorg Mansion. The Sorgs, a powerful and wealthy industrial family dating back to the nineteenth century, operated a large paper mill in Middletown. They donated enough money to put their names on the local opera house and helped build Middletown into a respectable enough city to attract Armco. Their mansion, a gigantic manor home, sits near a formerly proud Middletown country club. Despite its beauty, a Maryland couple recently purchased the mansion for $225,000, or about half of what a decent multi-room apartment sets you back in Washington, D.C.

Located quite literally on Main Street, the Sorg Mansion is just up the road from a number of opulent homes that housed Middletown's wealthy in their heyday. Most have fallen into disrepair. Those that haven't have been subdivided into small apartments for Middletown's poorest residents. A street that was once the pride of Middletown today serves as a meeting spot for druggies and dealers. Main Street is now the place you avoid after dark.

This change is a symptom of a new economic reality: rising residential segregation. The number of working-class whites in high-poverty neighborhoods is growing. In 1970, 25 percent of white children lived in a neighborhood with poverty rates above 10 percent. In 2000, that number was 40 percent. It's almost certainly even higher today. As a 2011 Brookings Institution study found, "compared to 2000, residents of extreme-poverty neighborhoods in 2005–09 were more likely to be white, native-born, high school or college graduates, homeowners, and not receiving public assistance."[12] In other words, bad neighborhoods no longer plague only urban ghettos; the bad neighborhoods have spread to the suburbs.

This has occurred for complicated reasons. Federal housing policy has actively encouraged homeownership, from Jimmy Carter's Community Reinvestment Act to George W. Bush's ownership society. But in the Middletowns of the world, homeownership comes at a steep social cost: As jobs disappear in a given area, declining home values trap people in certain neighborhoods. Even if you'd like to move, you can't, because the bottom has fallen out of the market—you now owe more than any buyer is willing to pay. The costs of moving are so high that many people stay put. Of course, the people trapped are usually those with the least money; those who can afford to leave do so.

City leaders have tried in vain to revive Middletown's downtown. You'll find their most infamous effort if you follow Central Avenue to its end point on the banks of the Miami River, once a lovely place. For reasons I can't begin to fathom, the city's brain trust decided to turn our beautiful riverfront into Lake Middletown, an infrastructural project that apparently involved shoveling tons of dirt into the river and hoping something interesting would come of it. It accomplished nothing, though the river now features a man-made dirt island about the size of a city block.

Efforts to reinvent downtown Middletown always struck me as futile. People didn't leave because our downtown lacked trendy cultural amenities. The trendy cultural amenities left because there weren't enough consumers in Middletown to support them.

And why weren't there enough well-paying consumers? Because there weren't enough jobs to employ those consumers. Downtown Middletown's struggles were a symptom of everything else happening to Middletown's people, especially the collapsing importance of Armco Kawasaki Steel.

AK Steel is the result of a 1989 merger between Armco Steel and Kawasaki—the same Japanese corporation that makes those small high-powered motorcycles ("crotch rockets," we called them as kids). Most people still call it Armco for two reasons. The first is that, as Mamaw used to say, "Armco built this fucking town." She wasn't lying: Many of the city's best parks and facilities were bought with Armco dollars. Armco's people sat on the boards of many of the important local organizations, and it helped to fund the schools. And it employed thousands of Middletonians who, like my grandfather, earned a good wage despite a lack of formal education.

Armco earned its reputation through careful design. "Until the 1950s," writes Chad Berry in his book *Southern Migrants, Northern Exiles,* "the 'big four' employers of the Miami Valley region—Procter and Gamble in Cincinnati, Champion Paper and Fiber in Hamilton, Armco Steel in Middletown, and National Cash Register in Dayton—had had serene labor relations, partly because they . . . [hired] family and friends of employees who were once migrants themselves. For example, Inland Container, in Middletown, had 220 Kentuckyians on its payroll, 117 of whom were from Wolfe County alone." While labor relations no doubt had declined by the 1980s, much of the goodwill built by Armco (and similar companies) remained.

The other reason most still call it Armco is that Kawasaki was a Japanese company, and in a town full of World War II vets and their families, you'd have thought that General Tojo himself had decided to set up shop in southwest Ohio when the merger was announced. The opposition was mostly a bunch of noise. Even Papaw—who once promised he'd disown his children if they bought a Japanese car—stopped complaining a few days after they announced the merger. "The truth is," he told me, "that the Japanese are our friends now. If we end up fighting any of those countries, it'll be the goddamned Chinese."

The Kawasaki merger represented an inconvenient truth: Manufacturing in America was a tough business in the post-globalization world. If companies like Armco were going to survive, they would have to retool. Kawasaki gave Armco a chance, and Middletown's flagship company probably would not have survived without it.

Growing up, my friends and I had no clue that the world had changed. Papaw had retired only a few years earlier, owned stock in Armco, and had a lucrative pension. Armco Park remained the nicest, most exclusive recreation spot in town, and access to the private park was a status symbol: It meant that your dad (or grandpa) was a man with a respected job. It never occurred to me that Armco wouldn't be around forever, funding scholarships, building parks, and throwing free concerts.

Still, few of my friends had ambitions to work there. As small children, we had the same dreams that other kids did; we wanted to be astronauts or football players or action heroes. I wanted to be a professional puppy-player-wither, which at the time seemed eminently reasonable. By the sixth grade, we wanted to be veterinarians or doctors or preachers or businessmen. But not steelworkers. Even at Roosevelt Elementary—where, thanks to Middletown geography, most people's parents lacked a college education—no one wanted to have a blue-collar career and its promise of a respectable middle-class life. We never considered that we'd be lucky to land a job at Armco; we took Armco for granted.

Many kids seem to feel that way today. A few years ago I spoke with Jennifer McGuffey, a Middletown High School teacher who works with at-risk youth. "A lot of students just don't understand what's out there," she told me, shaking her head. "You have the kids who plan on being baseball players but don't even play on the high school team because the coach is mean to them. Then you have those who aren't doing very well in school, and when you try to talk to them about what they're going to do, they talk about AK. 'Oh, I can get a job at AK. My uncle works there.' It's like they can't make the connection between the situation in this town and the lack of jobs at AK." My initial reaction was: How could these kids not understand what the world was like? Didn't they notice their town changing before their very eyes? But then I realized: We didn't, so why would they?

For my grandparents, Armco was an economic savior— the engine that brought them from the hills of Kentucky into America's middle class. My grandfather loved the company and knew every make and model of car built from Armco steel. Even after most American car companies transitioned away from steel-bodied cars, Papaw would stop at used-car dealerships whenever he saw an old Ford or Chevy. "Armco made this steel," he'd tell me. It was one of the few times that he ever betrayed a sense of genuine pride.

Despite that pride, he had no interest in my working there: "Your generation will make its living with their minds, not their hands," he once told me. The only acceptable career at Armco was as an engineer, not as a laborer in the weld shop. A lot of other Middletown parents and grandparents must have felt similarly: To them, the American Dream required forward momentum. Manual labor was honorable work, but it was their generation's work—we had to do something different. To move up was to move on. That required going to college.

And yet there was no sense that failing to achieve higher education would bring shame or any other consequences. The message wasn't explicit; teachers didn't tell us that we were too stupid or poor to make it. Nevertheless, it was all around us, like the air we breathed: No one in our families had gone to college; older friends and siblings were perfectly content to stay in Middletown, regardless of their career prospects; we knew no one at a prestigious out-of-state school; and everyone knew at least one young adult who was underemployed or didn't have a job at all.

In Middletown, 20 percent of the public high school's entering freshmen won't make it to graduation. Most won't graduate from college. Virtually no one will go to college out of state. Students don't expect much from themselves, because the people around them don't do very much. Many parents go along with this phenomenon. I don't remember ever being scolded for getting a bad grade until Mamaw began to take an interest in my grades in high school. When my sister or I struggled in school, I'd overhear things like "Well, maybe she's just not that great at fractions," or "J.D.'s more of a numbers kid, so I wouldn't worry about that spelling test."

There was, and still is, a sense that those who make it are of two varieties. The first are lucky: They come from wealthy families with connections, and their lives were set from the moment they were born. The second are the meritocratic: They were born with brains and couldn't fail if they tried. Because very few in Middletown fall into the former category, people assume that everyone who makes it is just really smart. To the average Middletonian, hard work doesn't matter as much as raw talent.

It's not like parents and teachers never mention hard work. Nor do they walk around loudly proclaiming that they expect their children to turn out poorly. These attitudes lurk below the surface, less in what people say than in how they act. One of our neighbors was a lifetime welfare recipient, but in between asking my grandmother to borrow her car or offering to trade food stamps for cash at a premium, she'd blather on about the importance of industriousness. "So many people abuse the system, it's impossible for the hardworking people to get the help they need," she'd say. This was the construct she'd built in her head: Most of the beneficiaries of the system were extravagant moochers, but she—despite never having worked in her life—was an obvious exception.

People talk about hard work all the time in places like Middletown. You can walk through a town where 30 percent of the young men work fewer than twenty hours a week and find not a single person aware of his own laziness. During the 2012 election cycle, the Public Religion Institute, a left-leaning think tank, published a report on working-class whites. It found, among other things, that working-class whites worked more hours than college-educated whites. But the idea that the average working-class white works more hours is demonstrably false.[13] The Public Religion Institute based its results on surveys—essentially, they called around and asked people what they thought.[14] The only thing that report proves is that many folks talk about working more than they actually work.

Of course, the reasons poor people aren't working as much as others are complicated, and it's too easy to blame the problem on laziness. For many, part-time work is all they have access to, because the Armcos of the world are going out of business and their skill sets don't fit well in the modern economy. But whatever the reasons, the rhetoric of hard work conflicts with the reality on the ground. The kids in Middletown absorb that conflict and struggle with it.

In this, as in so much else, the Scots-Irish migrants resemble their kin back in the holler. In an HBO documentary about eastern Kentucky hill people, the patriarch of a large Appalachian family introduces himself by drawing strict lines between work acceptable for men and work acceptable for women. While it's obvious what he considers "women's work," it's not at all clear what work, if any, is acceptable for him. Apparently not paid employment, since the man has never worked a paying job in his life. Ultimately, the verdict of his own son is damning: "Daddy says he's worked in his life. Only thing Daddy's worked is his goddamned ass. Why not be straight about it, Pa? Daddy was an alcoholic. He would stay drunk, he didn't bring food home. Mommy supported her young'uns. If it hadn't been for Mommy, we'd have been dead."[15]

Alongside these conflicting norms about the value of blue-collar work existed a massive ignorance about how to achieve white-collar work. We didn't know that all across the country—and even in our hometown—other kids had already started a competition to get ahead in life. During first grade, we played a game every morning: The teacher would announce the number of the day, and we'd go person by person and announce a math equation that produced the number. So if the number of the day was four, you could announce "two plus two" and claim a prize, usually a small piece of candy. One day the number was thirty. The students in front of me went through the easy answers—"twenty-nine plus one," "twenty-eight plus two," "fifteen plus fifteen." I was better than that. I was going to blow the teacher away.

When my turn came, I proudly announced, "Fifty minus twenty." The teacher gushed, and I received two pieces of candy for my foray into subtraction, a skill we'd learned only days before. A few moments later, while I beamed over my brilliance, another student announced, "Ten *times* three." I had no idea what that even meant. *Times?* Who was this guy?

The teacher was even more impressed, and my competitor triumphantly collected not two but three pieces of candy. The teacher spoke briefly of multiplication and asked if anyone else knew such a thing existed. None of us raised a hand. For my part, I was crushed. I returned home and burst into tears. I was certain my ignorance was rooted in some failure of character. I just felt *stupid*.

It wasn't my fault that until that day I had never heard the word "multiplication." It wasn't something I'd learned in school, and my family didn't sit around and work on math problems. But to a little kid who wanted to do well in school, it was a crushing defeat. In my immature brain, I didn't understand the difference between intelligence and knowledge. So I assumed I was an idiot.

I may not have known multiplication that day, but when I came home and told Papaw about my heartbreak, he turned it into triumph. I learned multiplication and division before dinner. And for two years after that, my grandfather and I would practice increasingly complex math once a week, with an ice cream reward for solid performance. I would beat myself up when I didn't understand a concept, and storm off, defeated. But after I'd pout for a few minutes, Papaw was always ready to go again. Mom was never much of a math person, but she took me to the public library before I could read, got me a library card, showed me how to use it, and always made sure I had access to kids' books at home.

In other words, despite all of the environmental pressures from my neighborhood and community, I received a different message at home. And that just might have saved me.

Chapter 5

I assume I'm not alone in having few memories from before I was six or seven. I know that I was four when I climbed on top of the dining room table in our small apartment, announced that I was the Incredible Hulk, and dove headfirst into the wall to prove that I was stronger than any building. (I was wrong.)

I remember being smuggled into the hospital to see Uncle Teaberry. I remember sitting on Mamaw Blanton's lap as she read Bible stories aloud before the sun came up, and I remember stroking the whiskers on her chin and wondering whether God gave all old women facial hair. I remember explaining to Ms. Hydorne in the holler that my name was "J.D., like jay-dot-dee-dot." I remember watching Joe Montana lead a TD-winning drive in the Super Bowl against the hometown Bengals. And I remember the early September day in kindergarten when Mom and Lindsay picked me up from school and told me that I'd never see my dad again. He was giving me up for adoption, they said. It was the saddest I had ever felt.

My father, Don Bowman, was Mom's second husband. Mom and Dad married in 1983 and split up around the time I started walking. Mom remarried a couple years after the divorce. Dad gave me up for adoption when I was six. After the adoption, he became kind of a phantom for the next six years. I had few memories of life with him. I knew that he loved Kentucky, its beautiful mountains, and its rolling green horse country. He drank RC Cola and had a clear Southern accent. He drank, but he stopped after he converted to Pentecostal Christianity. I always felt loved when I spent time with him, which was why I found it so shocking that he "didn't want me anymore," as Mom and Mamaw told me. He had a new wife, with two small children, and I'd been replaced.

Bob Hamel, my stepdad and eventual adoptive father, was a good guy in that he treated Lindsay and me kindly. Mamaw didn't care much for him. "He's a toothless fucking retard," she'd tell Mom, I suspect for reasons of class and culture: Mamaw had done everything in her power to be better than the circumstances of her birth. Though she was hardly rich, she wanted her kids to get an education, obtain white-collar work, and marry well-groomed middle-class folks—people, in other words, who were nothing like Mamaw and Papaw. Bob, however, was a walking hillbilly stereotype. He had little relationship with his own father and had learned the lessons of his own childhood well: He had two kids whom he barely saw, though they lived in Hamilton, a town ten miles south of Middletown. Half of his teeth had rotted out, and the other half were black, brown, and misshapen, the consequence of a lifetime of Mountain Dew consumption and presumably some missed dental checkups. He was a high school dropout who drove a truck for a living.

We'd all eventually learn that there was much to dislike about Bob. But what drove Mamaw's initial dislike were the parts of him that most resembled her. Mamaw apparently understood what would take me another twenty years to learn: that social class in America isn't just about money. And her desire that her children do better than she had done extended past their education and employment and into the relationships they formed. When it came to spouses for her kids and parents for her grandkids, Mamaw felt, whether she knew it consciously, that she wasn't good enough.

When Bob became my legal father, Mom changed my name from James Donald Bowman to James David Hamel. Until then, I'd borne my father's first name as my middle name, and Mom used the adoption to erase any memory of his existence. She kept the D to preserve what had by then become a universal nickname—J.D. Mom told me that I was now named after Uncle David, Mamaw's older, pot-smoking brother. This seemed a bit of a stretch even when I was six. Any old D name would have done, so long as it wasn't Donald.

Our new life with Bob had a superficial, family-sitcom feel to it. Mom and Bob's marriage seemed happy. They bought a house a few blocks away from Mamaw's. (We were so close that if the bathrooms were occupied or I felt like a snack, I'd just walk over to Mamaw's.) Mom had recently acquired her nursing license, and Bob made a great salary, so we had plenty of money. With our gun-toting, cigarette-smoking Mamaw up the street and a new legal father, we were an odd family but a happy one.

My life assumed a predictable cadence: I'd go to school and come home and eat dinner. I visited Mamaw and Papaw nearly every day. Papaw would sit on our porch to smoke, and I'd sit out there with him and listen to him grumble about politics or the steelworkers' union. When I learned to read, Mom bought me my first chapter book—*Space Brat*—and heaped praise on me for finishing it quickly. I loved to read, and I loved to work on math problems with Papaw, and I loved the way that Mom seemed to delight in everything I did.

Mom and I bonded over other things, especially our favorite sport: football. I read every word I could about Joe Montana, the greatest quarterback of all time, watched every game, and wrote fan mail to the 49ers and later the Chiefs, Montana's two teams. Mom checked out books on football strategy from the public library, and we built little models of the field with construction paper and loose change—pennies for the defense, nickels and dimes for the offense.

Mom didn't want me to understand only the rules of football; she wanted me to understand the strategy. We practiced on our construction-paper football field, going over the various contingencies: What happened if a particular lineman (a shiny nickel) missed his block? What could the quarterback (a dime) do if no receiver (another dime) was open? We didn't have chess, but we did have football.

More than anyone else in my family, Mom wanted us to be exposed to people from all walks of life. Her friend Scott was a kind old gay man who, she later told me, died unexpectedly. She made me watch a movie about Ryan White, a boy not that much older than I was, who contracted HIV through a blood transfusion and had to start a legal fight to return to school. Every time I complained about school, Mom reminded me of Ryan White and spoke about what a blessing it was to get an education. She was so overcome by White's story that she handwrote a letter to his mother after he died in 1990.

Mom believed deeply in the promise of education. She was the salutatorian of her high school class but never made it to college because Lindsay was born weeks after Mom graduated from high school. But she did return to a local community college and earn an associate's degree in nursing. I was probably seven or eight when she started working full-time as a nurse, and I liked to think that I had contributed in some small way: I "helped" her study by crawling all over her, and I let her practice drawing blood on my youthful veins.

Sometimes Mom's devotion to education arguably went a little too far. During my third-grade science fair project, Mom helped at every stage—from planning the project to assisting with lab notes to assembling the presentation. The night before everything was due, the project looked precisely how it deserved to look: like the work of a third-grader who had slacked off a bit. I went to bed expecting to wake up the next morning, give my mediocre presentation, and call it a day. The science fair was a competition, and I even thought that, with a little salesmanship, I could advance to the next round. But in the morning I discovered that Mom had revamped the entire presentation. It looked like a scientist and a professional artist had joined forces to create it. Though the judges were blown away, when they began to ask questions that I couldn't answer (but that the maker of the collage would have known), they realized something didn't fit. I didn't make it to the final round of the competition.

What that incident taught me—besides the fact that I needed to do my own work—was that Mom cared deeply about enterprises of the mind. Nothing brought her greater joy than when I finished a book or asked for another. Mom was, everyone told me, the smartest person they knew. And I believed it. She was definitely the smartest person I knew.

In the southwest Ohio of my youth, we learned to value loyalty, honor, and toughness. I earned my first bloody nose at five and my first black eye at six. Each of these fights began after someone insulted my mother. Mother jokes were never allowed, and grandmother jokes earned the harshest punishment that my little fists could administer. Mamaw and Papaw ensured that I knew the basic rules of fighting: You never start a fight; you always end the fight if someone else starts it; and even though you never start a fight, it's maybe okay to start one if a man insults your family. This last rule was unspoken but clear. Lindsay had a boyfriend named Derrick, maybe her first boyfriend, who broke up with her after a few days. She was heartbroken as only thirteen-year-olds can be, so I decided to confront Derrick when I saw him walking past our house one day. He had five years and about thirty-five pounds on me, but I came at him twice as he pushed me down easily. The third time I came at him, he'd had enough and proceeded to pound the shit out of me. I ran to Mamaw's house for some first aid, crying and a little bloody. She just smiled at me. "You did good, honey. You did real good."

In fighting, as with many things, Mamaw taught me through experience. She never laid a hand on me punitively—she was anti-spanking in a way must have come from her own bad experiences—but when I asked her what it felt like to be punched in the head, she showed me. A swift blow, delivered by the meat of her hand, directly on my cheek. "That didn't feel so bad, did it?" And the answer was no. Getting hit in the face wasn't nearly as terrible as I'd imagined. This was one of her most important rules of fighting: Unless someone really knows how to hit, a punch in the face is no big deal. Better to take a blow to the face than to miss an opportunity to deliver your own. Her second tip was to stand sideways, with your left shoulder facing your opponent and your hands raised because "you're a much smaller target that way." Her third rule was to punch with your whole body, especially your hips. Very few people, Mamaw told me, appreciate how unimportant your fist is when it comes to hitting someone.

Despite her admonition not to start fights, our unspoken honor code made it easy to convince someone else to start a fight for you. If you really wanted to get into it with someone, all you needed to do was insult his mom. No amount of self-control could withstand a well-played maternal criticism. "Your mom's so fat that her ass has its own zip code"; "Your mom's such a hillbilly that her false teeth have cavities"; or a simple "Yo' mama!" These were fighting words, whether you wanted them to be or not. To shirk from avenging a string of insults was to lose your honor, your dignity, or even your friends. It was to go home and be afraid to tell your family that you had disgraced them.

I don't know why, but after a few years Mamaw's views evolved on fighting. I was in third grade, had just lost a race, and felt there was only one way to adequately deal with the taunting victor. Mamaw, lurking nearby, intervened in what was certain to be another schoolyard cage match. She sternly asked whether I had forgotten her lesson that the only just fights are defensive. I didn't know what to say—she had endorsed the unstated rule of honor fighting only a few years earlier. "One time I got in a fight and you told me that I did good," I told her. She said, "Well, then, I was wrong. You shouldn't fight unless you have to." Now, *that* made an impression. Mamaw never admitted mistakes.

The next year, I noticed that a class bully had taken a particular interest in a specific victim, an odd kid I rarely spoke to. Thanks to my prior exploits, I was largely immune to bullying, and, like most kids, was usually content to avoid the bully's attention. One day, though, he said something about his victim that I overheard, and I felt a strong urge to stick up for the poor kid. There was something pathetic about the target, who seemed especially wounded by the bully's treatment.

When I spoke to Mamaw after school that day, I broke down in tears. I felt incredibly guilty that I hadn't had the courage to speak up for this poor kid—that I had just sat there and listened to someone else make his life a living hell. She asked whether I had spoken to the teacher about it, and I assured her that I had. "That bitch ought to be put in jail for sitting there and not doing anything." And then she said something that I will never forget: "Sometimes, honey, you have to fight, even when you're not defending yourself. Sometimes it's just the right thing to do. Tomorrow you need to stand up for that boy, and if you have to stand up for yourself, then do that, too." Then she taught me a move: a swift, hard (make sure to turn your hips) punch right to the gut. "If he starts in on you, make sure to punch him right in the belly button."

The next day at school, I felt nervous and hoped that the bully would take a day off. But in the predictable chaos as the class lined up for lunch, the bully—his name was Chris—asked my little charge whether he planned on crying that day. "Shut up," I said. "Just leave him alone." Chris approached me, pushed me, and asked what I planned to do about it. I walked right up to him, pivoted my right hip, and sucker-punched him right in the stomach. He immediately—and terrifyingly—dropped to his knees, seemingly unable to breathe. By the time I realized that I'd really injured him, he was alternately coughing and trying to catch his breath. He even spit up a small amount of blood.

Chris went to the school nurse, and after I confirmed that I hadn't killed him and would avoid the police, my thoughts immediately turned to the school justice system—whether I'd be suspended or expelled and for how long. While the other kids played at recess and Chris recovered with the nurse, the teacher brought me into the classroom. I thought she was going to tell me that she'd called my parents and I'd be kicked out of school. Instead, she gave me a lecture about fighting and made me practice my handwriting instead of playing outside. I detected a hint of approval from the teacher, and I sometimes wonder whether there were school politics at work in her inability to appropriately discipline the class bully. At any rate, Mamaw found out about the fight directly from me and praised me for doing something really good. It was the last time I ever got in a fistfight.

While I recognized that things weren't perfect, I also recognized that our family shared a lot with most of the families I saw around me. Yes, my parents fought intensely, but so did everyone else's. Yes, my grandparents played as big a role in my life as Mom and Bob did, but that was the norm in hillbilly families. We didn't live a peaceful life in a small nuclear family. We lived a chaotic life in big groups of aunts, uncles, grandparents, and cousins. This was the life I'd been given, and I was a pretty happy kid.

When I was about nine years old, things began to unravel at home. Tired of Papaw's constant presence and Mamaw's "interference," Mom and Bob decided to move to Preble County, a sparsely populated part of Ohio farm country approximately thirty-five miles from Middletown. Even as a boy, I knew this was the very worst thing that could happen to me. Mamaw and

Papaw were my best friends. They helped me with my homework and spoiled me with treats when I behaved correctly or finished a difficult school assignment. They were also the gatekeepers. They were the scariest people I knew—old hillbillies who carried loaded guns in their coat pockets and under their car seats, no matter the occasion. They kept the monsters at bay.

Bob was Mom's third husband, but the third time was not the charm. By the time we moved to Preble County, Mom and Bob had already begun to fight, and many of those fights would keep me up well past my bedtime. They said things friends and family should never say to each other: "Fuck you!" "Go back to your trailer park," Mom sometimes told Bob, a reference to his life before they were married. Sometimes Mom would take us to a local motel, where we'd hide out for a few days until Mamaw or Papaw convinced Mom to face her domestic problems.

Mom had a lot of Mamaw's fire, which meant that she never allowed herself to become a victim during domestic disputes. It also meant that she often escalated normal disagreements beyond where they should go. During one of my second-grade football games, a tall, overweight mother muttered about why I had been given the ball on the previous play. Mom, a bleacher row behind the woman, overheard the comment and told her that I'd been given the ball because, unlike her child, I wasn't a fat piece of shit who'd been raised by a fat piece-of-shit mother. By the time I observed the commotion on the sidelines, Bob was ripping Mom away with the woman's hair still clenched in her hands. After the game, I asked Mom what happened, and she replied only, "No one criticizes my boy." I beamed with pride.

In Preble County, with Mamaw and Papaw over forty-five minutes away, the fights turned into screaming matches. Often the subject was money, though it made little sense for a rural Ohio family with a combined income of over a hundred thousand dollars to struggle with money. But fight they did, because they bought things they didn't need—new cars, new trucks, a swimming pool. By the time their short marriage fell apart, they were tens of thousands of dollars in debt, with nothing to show for it.

Finances were the least of our problems. Mom and Bob had never been violent with each other, but that slowly started to change. I awoke one night to the sound of breaking glass—Mom had lobbed plates at Bob—and ran downstairs to see what was up. He was holding her against the kitchen counter, and she was flailing and biting at him. When she dropped to the ground, I ran to her lap. When Bob moved closer, I stood up and punched him in the face. He reared back (to return the blow, I figured), and I collapsed on the ground with my arms over my head in anticipation. The blow never came—Bob never was physically abusive—and my intervention somehow ended the fight. He walked over to the couch and sat down silently, staring at the wall; Mom and I meekly walked upstairs to bed.

Mom and Bob's problems were my first introduction to marital conflict resolution. Here were the takeaways: Never speak at a reasonable volume when screaming will do; if the fight gets a little too intense, it's okay to slap and punch, so long as the man doesn't hit first; always express your feelings in a way that's insulting and hurtful to your partner; if all else fails, take the kids and the dog to a local motel, and don't tell your spouse where to find you—if he or she knows where the children are, he or she won't worry as much, and your departure won't be as effective.

I began to do poorly in school. Many nights I'd lie in bed, unable to sleep because of the noise—the furniture rocking, heavy stomping, yelling, sometimes glass shattering. The next morning I'd wake up tired and depressed, meandering through the school day, thinking constantly about what awaited at home. I just wanted to retreat to a place where I could sit in silence. I couldn't tell anyone what was going on, as that was far too embarrassing. And though I hated school, I hated home more. When the teacher announced that we had only a few minutes to clear our desks before the bell rang, my heart sank. I'd stare at the clock as if it were a ticking bomb. Not even Mamaw understood how terrible things had become. My slipping grades were the first indication.

Not every day was like that, of course. But even when the house was ostensibly peaceful, our lives were so charged that I was constantly on guard. Mom and Bob never smiled at each other or said nice things to Lindsay and me anymore. You never knew when the wrong word would turn a quiet dinner into a terrible fight, or when a minor childhood transgression would send a plate or book flying across the room. It was like we were living among land mines—one wrong step, and *kaboom*.

Up to that point in my life, I was a perfectly fit and healthy child. I exercised constantly, and though I didn't exactly watch what I ate, I didn't have to. But I began to put on weight, and I was positively chubby by the time I started the fifth grade. I often felt sick and would complain of severe stomachaches to the school nurse. Though I didn't realize it at the time, the trauma at home was clearly affecting my health. "Elementary students may show signs of distress through somatic complaints such as stomachaches, headaches, and pains," reads one resource for school administrators who deal with children who suffer trauma at home. "These students may have a change in behavior, such as increased irritability, aggression, and anger. Their behaviors may be inconsistent. These students may show a change in school performance and have impaired attention and concentration and more school absences." I just thought I was constipated or that I really hated my new hometown.

Mom and Bob weren't that abnormal. It would be tough to chronicle all the outbursts and screaming matches I witnessed that had nothing to do with my family. My neighbor friend and I would play in his backyard until we heard screaming from his parents, and then we'd run into the alley and hide. Papaw's neighbors would yell so loudly that we could hear it from inside his house, and it was so common that he'd always say, "Goddammit, there they go again." I once saw a young couple's argument at the local Chinese buffet escalate into a symphony of curse words and insults. Mamaw and I used to open the windows on one side of her house so we could hear the substance of the explosive fights between her neighbor Pattie and Pattie's boyfriend. Seeing people insult, scream, and sometimes physically fight was just a part of our life. After a while, you didn't even notice it.

I always thought it was how adults spoke to one another. When Lori married Dan, I learned of at least one exception. Mamaw told me that Dan and Aunt Wee never screamed at each other because Dan was different. "He's a saint," she'd say. As we got to know Dan's entire family, I realized that they were just nicer to each other. They didn't yell at each other in public. I got the distinct impression that they didn't yell at each other much in private, either. I thought they were frauds. Aunt Wee saw it differently. "I just assumed they were really weird. I knew they were genuine. I just figured they were genuinely odd."

The never-ending conflict took its toll. Even thinking about it today makes me nervous. My heart begins to race, and my stomach leaps into my throat. When I was very young, all I wanted to do was get away from it—to hide from the fighting, go to Mamaw's, or disappear. I couldn't hide from it, because it was all around me.

Over time, I started to like the drama. Instead of hiding from it, I'd run downstairs or put my ear to the wall to get a better listen. My heart would still race, but in an anticipatory way, like it did when I was about to score in a basketball game. Even the fight that went too far—when I thought Bob was about to hit me—was less about a brave kid who intervened and more about a spectator who got a little too close to the action. This thing that I hated had become a sort of drug.

One day I came home from school to see Mamaw's car in the driveway. It was an ominous sign, as she never made unannounced visits to our Preble County home. She made an exception on this day because Mom was in the hospital, the result of a failed suicide attempt. For all the things I saw happening in the world around me, my eleven-year-old eyes missed so much. In her work at Middletown Hospital, Mom had met and fallen in love with a local fireman and begun a years-long affair. That morning Bob had confronted her about the affair and demanded a divorce. Mom had sped off in her brand-new minivan and intentionally crashed it into a telephone pole. That's what she said, at least. Mamaw had her own theory: that Mom had tried to detract attention from her cheating and financial problems. As Mamaw said, "Who tries to kill themselves by crashing a fucking car? If she wanted to kill herself, I've got plenty of guns."

Lindsay and I largely bought Mamaw's view of things, and

we felt relief more than anything—that Mom hadn't really hurt herself, and that Mom's attempted suicide would be the end of our Preble County experiment. She spent only a couple days in the hospital. Within a month, we moved back to Middletown, one block closer to Mamaw than we'd been before, with one less man in tow.

Despite the return to a familiar home, Mom's behavior grew increasingly erratic. She was more roommate than parent, and of the three of us—Mom, Lindsay, and me—Mom was the roommate most prone to hard living. I'd go to bed only to wake up around midnight, when Lindsay got home from doing whatever teenagers do. I'd wake up again at two or three in the morning, when Mom got home. She had new friends, most of them younger and without kids. And she cycled through boyfriends, switching partners every few months. It was so bad that my best friend at the time commented on her "flavors of the month." I'd grown accustomed to a certain amount of instability, but it was of a familiar type: There would be fighting or running away from fights; when things got rocky, Mom would explode on us or even slap or pinch us. I didn't like it—who would?—but this new behavior was just strange. Though Mom had been many things, she hadn't been a partier. When we moved back to Middletown, that changed.

With partying came alcohol, and with alcohol came alcohol abuse and even more bizarre behavior. One day when I was about twelve, Mom said something that I don't remember now, but I recall running out the door without my shoes and going to Mamaw's house. For two days, I refused to speak to or see my mother. Papaw, worried about the disintegrating relationship between his daughter and her son, begged me to see her.

So I listened to the apology that I'd heard a million times before. Mom was always good at apologies. Maybe she had to be—if she didn't say "sorry," then Lindsay and I never would have spoken to her. But I think she really meant it. Deep down, she always felt guilty about the things that happened, and she probably even believed that—as promised—they'd "never happen again." They always did, though.

This time was no different. Mom was extra-apologetic because her sin was extra-bad. So her penance was extra-good: She promised to take me to the mall and buy me football cards. Football cards were my kryptonite, so I agreed to join her. It was probably the biggest mistake of my life.

We got on the highway, and I said something that ignited her temper. So she sped up to what seemed like a hundred miles per hour and told me that she was going to crash the car and kill us both. I jumped into the backseat, thinking that if I could use two seat belts at once, I'd be more likely to survive the impact. This infuriated her more, so she pulled over to beat the shit out of me. When she did, I leaped out of the car and ran for my life. We were in a rural part of the state, and I ran through a large field of grass, the tall blades slapping my ankles as I sped away. I happened upon a small house with an aboveground pool. The owner—an overweight woman about the same age as Mom— was floating on her back, enjoying the nice June weather.

"You have to call my mamaw!" I screamed. "Please help me. My mom is trying to kill me." The woman clambered out of the pool as I looked around fearfully, terrified of any sign of my mother. We went inside, and I called Mamaw and repeated the woman's address. "Please hurry up," I told her. "Mom is going to find me."

Mom did find me. She must have seen where I ran from the highway. She banged on the door and demanded that I come out. I begged the owner not to open the door, so she locked the doors and promised Mom that her two dogs—each no bigger than a medium-sized house cat—would attack her if she tried to enter. Eventually Mom broke down the woman's door and dragged me out as I screamed and clutched for anything—the screen door, the guardrails on the steps, the grass on the ground. The woman stood there and watched, and I hated her for doing nothing. But she had in fact done something: In the minutes between my call to Mamaw and Mom's arrival, the woman had apparently dialed 911. So as Mom dragged me to her car, two police cruisers pulled up, and the cops who got out put Mom in handcuffs. She did not go quietly; they wrestled her into the back of a cruiser. Then she was gone.

The second cop put me in the back of his cruiser as we waited for Mamaw to arrive. I have never felt so lonely, watching that cop interview the homeowner—still in her soaking-wet bathing suit, flanked by two pint-sized guard dogs—unable to open the cruiser door from the inside, and unsure when I could expect Mamaw's arrival. I had begun to daydream when the car door swung open, and Lindsay crawled into the cruiser with me and clutched me to her chest so tightly that I couldn't breathe. We didn't cry; we said nothing. I just sat there being squeezed to death and feeling like all was right with the world.

When we got out of the car, Mamaw and Papaw hugged me and asked if I was okay. Mamaw spun me around to inspect me. Papaw spoke with the police officer about where to find his incarcerated daughter. Lindsay never let me out of her sight. It had been the scariest day of my life. But the hard part was over.

When we got home, none of us could talk. Mamaw wore a silent, terrifying anger. I hoped that she would calm down before Mom got out of jail. I was exhausted and wanted only to lie on the couch and watch TV. Lindsay went upstairs and took a nap. Papaw collected a food order for Wendy's. On his way to the front door, he stopped and stood over me on the couch. Mamaw had left the room temporarily. Papaw placed his hand on my forehead and began to sob. I was so afraid that I didn't even look up at his face. I had never heard of him crying, never seen him cry, and assumed he was so tough that he hadn't even cried as a baby. He held that pose for a little while, until we both heard Mamaw approaching the living room. At that point he collected himself, wiped his eyes, and left. Neither of us ever spoke of that moment.

Mom was released from jail on bond and prosecuted for a domestic violence misdemeanor. The case depended entirely on me. Yet during the hearing, when asked if Mom had ever threatened me, I said no. The reason was simple: My grandparents were paying a lot of money for the town's highest-powered lawyer. They were furious with my mother, but they didn't want their daughter in jail, either. The lawyer never explicitly encouraged dishonesty, but he did make it clear that what I said would either increase or decrease the odds that Mom spent additional time in prison. "You don't want your mom to go to jail, do you?" he asked. So I lied, with the express understanding that even though Mom would have her liberty, I could live with my grandparents whenever I wished. Mom would officially retain custody, but from that day forward I lived in her house only when I chose to—and Mamaw told me that if Mom had a problem with the arrangement, she could talk to the barrel of Mamaw's gun. This was hillbilly justice, and it didn't fail me.

I remember sitting in that busy courtroom, with half a dozen other families all around, and thinking they looked just like us. The moms and dads and grandparents didn't wear suits like the lawyers and judge. They wore sweatpants and stretchy pants and T-shirts. Their hair was a bit frizzy. And it was the first time I noticed "TV accents"—the neutral accent that so many news anchors had. The social workers and the judge and the lawyer all had TV accents. None of us did. The people who ran the courthouse were different from us. The people subjected to it were not.

Identity is an odd thing, and I didn't understand at the time why I felt such kinship with these strangers. A few months later, during my first trip to California, I began to understand. Uncle Jimmy flew Lindsay and me to his home in Napa, California. Knowing that I'd be visiting him, I told every person I could that I was headed to California in the summer and, what was more, flying for the first time. The main reaction was disbelief that my uncle had enough money to fly two people—neither of whom were his children—out to California. It is a testament to the class consciousness of my youth that my friends' thoughts drifted first to the cost of an airplane flight.

For my part, I was overjoyed to travel west and visit Uncle Jimmy, a man I idolized on par with my great-uncles, the Blanton men. Despite the early departure, I didn't sleep a wink on the six-hour flight from Cincinnati to San Francisco. Everything was just too exciting: the way the earth shrank during takeoff, the look of clouds from close up, the scope and size of the sky, and the way the mountains looked from the stratosphere. The flight attendant took notice, and by the time we hit Colorado, I was making regular visits to the cockpit (this was before 9/11), where the pilot gave me brief lessons in flying an airplane and updated me on our progress.

The adventure had just begun. I had traveled out of state before: I had joined my grandparents on road trips to South Carolina and Texas, and I visited Kentucky regularly. On those trips, I rarely spoke to anyone except family, and I never noticed anything all that different. Napa was like a different country. In California, every day included a new adventure with my teenage cousins and their friends. During one trip we went to the Castro District of San Francisco so that, in the words of my older cousin Rachael, I could learn that gay people weren't out to molest me. Another day, we visited a winery. On yet another day, we helped at my cousin Nate's high school football practice. It was all very exciting. Everyone I met thought I sounded like I was from Kentucky. Of course, I kind of was from Kentucky. And I loved that people thought I had a funny accent. That said, it became clear to me that California really was something else. I'd visited Pittsburgh, Cleveland, Columbus, and Lexington. I'd spent a considerable amount of time in South Carolina, Kentucky, Tennessee, and even Arkansas. So why was California so different?

The answer, I'd learn, was the same hillbilly highway that brought Mamaw and Papaw from eastern Kentucky to southwest Ohio. Despite the topographical differences and the different regional economies of the South and the industrial Midwest, my travels had been confined largely to places where the people looked and acted like my family. We ate the same foods, watched the same sports, and practiced the same religion. That's why I felt so much kinship with those people at the courthouse: They were hillbilly transplants in one way or another, just like me.

Chapter 6

One of the questions I loathed, and that adults always asked, was whether I had any brothers or sisters. When you're a kid, you can't wave your hand, say, "It's complicated," and move on. And unless you're a particularly capable sociopath, dishonesty can only take you so far. So, for a time, I dutifully answered, walking people through the tangled web of familial relationships that I'd grown accustomed to. I had a biological half brother and half sister whom I never saw because my biological father had given me up for adoption. I had many stepbrothers and stepsisters by one measure, but only two if you limited the tally to the offspring of Mom's husband of the moment. Then there was my biological dad's wife, and she had at least one kid, so maybe I should count him, too. Sometimes I'd wax philosophical about the meaning of the word "sibling": Are the children of your mom's previous husbands still related to you? If so, what about the future children of your mom's previous husbands? By some metrics, I probably had about a dozen stepsiblings.

There was one person for whom the term "sibling" definitely applied: my sister, Lindsay. If any adjective ever preceded her in-

troduction, it was always one of pride: "my *full* sister, Lindsay";
"my *whole* sister, Lindsay"; "my *big* sister, Lindsay." Lindsay was
(and remains) the person I was proudest to know. The moment
I learned that "half sister" had nothing to do with my affections
and everything to do with the genetic nature of our relationship—
that Lindsay, by virtue of having a different father, was just as
much my half sister as people I'd never seen—remains one of the
most devastating moments of my life. Mamaw told me this nonchalantly as I exited the shower one night before bedtime, and I
screamed and wailed as if I'd just learned that my dog had died. I
calmed down only after Mamaw relented and agreed that hence-
forth no one would ever refer to Lindsay as my "half sister" again.

Lindsay Leigh was five years older than I was, born just two
months after Mom graduated from high school. I was obsessed
with her, both in the way that all children adore their older siblings and in a way that was unique to our circumstances. Her
heroism on my behalf was the stuff of legend. One time after
she and I argued over a soft pretzel, leading Mom to drop me
off in an empty parking lot to show Lindsay what life without
me would look like, it was my sister's fit of sorrow and rage that
brought Mom back immediately. During explosive fights between Mom and whatever man she let into our home, it was
Lindsay who withdrew to her bedroom to place a rescue call to
Mamaw and Papaw. She fed me when I was hungry, changed my
diaper when no one else did, and dragged me everywhere with
her—even though, Mamaw and Aunt Wee told me, I weighed
nearly as much as she did.

I always saw her as more adult than child. She never expressed
her displeasure at her teenage boyfriends by storming off and
slamming doors. When Mom worked late nights or otherwise

didn't make it home, Lindsay ensured that we had something for dinner. I annoyed her, like all little brothers annoy their sisters, but she never yelled at me, screamed at me, or made me afraid of her. In one of my most shameful moments, I wrestled Lindsay to the ground for reasons I don't remember. I was ten or eleven, which would have made her about fifteen, and though I realized then that I'd outgrown her in terms of strength, I continued to think there was nothing childlike about her. She was above it all, the "one true adult in the house," as Papaw would say, and my first line of defense, even before Mamaw. She made dinner when she had to, did the laundry when no one else did, and rescued me from the backseat of that police cruiser. I depended on her so completely that I didn't see Lindsay for what she was: a young girl, not yet old enough to drive a car, learning to fend for herself and her little brother at the same time.

That began to change the day our family decided to give Lindsay a shot at her dreams. Lindsay had always been a beautiful girl. When my friends and I ranked the world's prettiest girls, I listed Lindsay first, just ahead of Demi Moore and Pam Anderson. Lindsay had learned of a modeling recruitment event at a Dayton hotel, so Mom, Mamaw, Lindsay, and I piled into Mamaw's Buick and headed north. Lindsay was bursting with excitement, and I was, too. This was going to be her big break and, by extension, our whole family's.

When we arrived at the hotel, a lady instructed us to follow signs to a giant ballroom and wait in line. The ballroom was perfectly tacky in that 1970s sort of way: ugly carpet, big chandeliers, and lighting just bright enough to prevent you from stumbling over your own feet. I wondered how any talent agent could ever appreciate my sister's beauty. It was too damned dark.

Eventually we reached the front of the line, and the talent agent seemed optimistic about my sister. She said something about how cute she was and told her to go wait in another room. Surprisingly, she said that I was model material, too, and asked if I'd like to follow my sister and hear about our next step. I agreed enthusiastically.

After a little while in the holding room, Lindsay and I and the other selectees learned that we had made it to the next round, but another trial awaited us in New York City. The agency employees gave us brochures with more information and told us that we needed to RSVP within the next few weeks. On the way home, Lindsay and I were ecstatic. We were going to New York City to become famous models.

The fee for traveling to New York was hefty, and if someone had really wanted us as models, they likely would have paid for our audition. In hindsight, the cursory treatment they gave each individual—each "audition" was no longer than a few-sentence conversation—suggests that the whole event was more scam than talent search. But I don't know: Model audition protocol has never been my area of expertise.

What I do know is that our exuberance didn't survive the car ride. Mom began to worry aloud about the cost of the trip, causing Lindsay and me to bicker about which one of us should go (no doubt I was being a brat). Mom became progressively angrier and then snapped. What happened next was no surprise: There was a lot of screaming, some punching and driving, and then a stopped car on the side of the road, full of two sobbing kids. Mamaw intervened before things got out of hand, but it's a miracle we didn't crash and die: Mom driving and slapping the kids in the backseat; Mamaw on the passenger side, slapping and screaming at Mom. That was why the car stopped—though Mom was a multitasker, this was too much. We drove home in silence after Mamaw explained that if Mom lost her temper again, Mamaw would shoot her in the face. That night we stayed at Mamaw's house.

I'll never forget Lindsay's face as she marched upstairs to bed. It wore the pain of a defeat known by only a person who experiences the highest high and the lowest low in a matter of minutes. She had been on the cusp of achieving a childhood dream; now she was just another teenage girl with a broken heart. Mamaw turned to retire to her couch, where she would watch *Law & Order*, read the Bible, and fall asleep. I stood in the narrow walkway that separated the living room from the dining room and asked Mamaw a question that had been on my mind since she ordered Mom to drive us home safely. I knew what she'd say, but I guess I just wanted reassurance. "Mamaw, does God love us?" She hung her head, gave me a hug, and began to cry.

The question wounded Mamaw because the Christian faith stood at the center of our lives, especially hers. We never went to church, except on rare occasions in Kentucky or when Mom decided that what we needed in our lives was religion. Nevertheless, Mamaw's was a deeply personal (albeit quirky) faith. She couldn't say "organized religion" without contempt. She saw churches as breeding grounds for perverts and money changers. And she hated what she called "the loud and proud"—people who wore their faith on their sleeve, always ready to let you know how pious they were. Still, she sent much of her spare income to churches in Jackson, Kentucky, especially those controlled by Reverend Donald Ison, an older man who bore a striking resemblance to the priest from *The Exorcist*.

By Mamaw's reckoning, God never left our side. He celebrated with us when times were good and comforted us when they weren't. During one of our many trips to Kentucky, Mamaw was trying to merge onto the highway after a brief stop for gas. She didn't pay attention to the signs, so we found ourselves headed the wrong way on a one-way exit ramp with angry motorists swerving out of our way. I was screaming in terror, but after a U-turn on a three-lane interstate, the only thing Mamaw said about the incident was "We're fine, goddammit. Don't you know Jesus rides in the car with me?"

The theology she taught was unsophisticated, but it provided a message I needed to hear. To coast through life was to squander my God-given talent, so I had to work hard. I had to take care of my family because Christian duty demanded it. I needed to forgive, not just for my mother's sake but for my own. I should never despair, for God had a plan.

Mamaw often told a parable: A young man was sitting at home when a terrible rainstorm began. Within hours, the man's house began to flood, and someone came to his door offering a ride to higher ground. The man declined, saying, "God will take care of me." A few hours later, as the waters engulfed the first floor of the man's home, a boat passed by, and the captain offered to take the man to safety. The man declined, saying, "God will take care of me." A few hours after that, as the man waited on his roof—his entire home flooded—a helicopter flew by, and the pilot offered transportation to dry land. Again the man declined, telling the pilot that God would care for him. Soon thereafter, the waters overcame the man, and as he stood before God in heaven, he protested his fate: "You promised that you'd help me so long as I was faithful." God replied, "I sent you a car, a boat, and a helicopter. Your death is your own fault." God helps those who help themselves. This was the wisdom of the Book of Mamaw.

The fallen world described by the Christian religion matched the world I saw around me: one where a happy car ride could quickly turn to misery, one where individual misconduct rippled across a family's and a community's life. When I asked Mamaw if God loved us, I asked her to reassure me that this religion of ours could still make sense of the world we lived in. I needed reassurance of some deeper justice, some cadence or rhythm that lurked beneath the heartache and chaos.

Not long after Lindsay's childhood modeling dream went up in flames, I was in Jackson with Mamaw and my cousin Gail on August 2, my eleventh birthday. Late in the afternoon, Mamaw advised me to call Bob—still my legal father—because I hadn't heard from him yet. After we moved back to Middletown, he and Mom divorced, so it wasn't surprising that he rarely got in touch. But my birthday was obviously special, and I found it odd that he hadn't called. So I phoned and got the answering machine. A few hours later, I phoned once more with the same result, and I knew instinctively that I would never see Bob again.

Either because she felt bad for me or because she knew I loved dogs, Gail took me to the local pet store, where a brand-new litter of German shepherd puppies was on display. I desperately wanted one and had just enough birthday money to make the purchase. Gail reminded me that dogs were a lot of work and that my family (read: my mother) had a terrible history of getting dogs and then giving them away. When wisdom fell on deaf ears—"You're probably right, Gail, but they're soooo cute!"—

authority kicked in: "Honey, I'm sorry, but I'm not letting you buy this dog." By the time we returned to Mamaw Blanton's house, I was more upset about the dog than about losing father number two.

I cared less about the fact that Bob was gone than about the disruption his departure would inevitably cause. He was just the latest casualty in a long line of failed paternal candidates. There was Steve, a soft-spoken man with a temperament to match. I used to pray that Mom would marry Steve because he was nice and had a good job. But they broke up, and she moved on to Chip, a local police officer. Chip was kind of a hillbilly himself: He loved cheap beer, country music, and catfish fishing, and we got along well until he, too, was gone.

One of the worst parts, honestly, was that Bob's departure would further complicate the tangled web of last names in our family. Lindsay was a Lewis (her dad's last name), Mom took the last name of whichever husband she was married to, Mamaw and Papaw were Vances, and all of Mamaw's brothers were Blantons. I shared a name with no one I really cared about (which bothered me already), and with Bob gone, explaining why my name was J.D. Hamel would require a few additional awkward moments. "Yeah, my legal father's last name is Hamel. You haven't met him because I don't see him. No, I don't know why I don't see him."

Of all the things that I hated about my childhood, nothing compared to the revolving door of father figures. To her credit, Mom had avoided abusive or neglectful partners, and I never felt mistreated by any of the men she brought into our home. But I hated the disruption. And I hated how often these boyfriends would walk out of my life just as I'd begun to like them. Lindsay, with the benefit of age and wisdom, viewed all of the men skeptically. She knew that at some point they'd be gone. With Bob's departure, I had learned the same lesson.

Mom brought these men into our lives for the right reasons. She often wondered aloud whether Chip or Bob or Steve made good "father figures." She would say: "He takes you fishing, which is really good" or "It's important to learn something about masculinity from someone closer to your age." When I heard her screaming at one of them, or weeping on the floor after an especially intense argument, or when I saw her mired in despair after a breakup, I felt guilty that she was going through this for my sake. After all, I thought, Papaw was plenty good as a father figure. I promised her after each breakup that we would be okay or that we'd get over this together or (echoing Mamaw) that we didn't need any damned men. I know Mom's motives were not entirely selfless: She (like all of us) was motivated by the desire for love and companionship. But she was looking out for us, too.

The road to hell, however, is paved with good intentions. Caught between various dad candidates, Lindsay and I never learned how a man should treat a woman. Chip may have taught me how to tie a fishing hook, but I learned little else about what masculinity required of me other than drinking beer and screaming at a woman when she screamed at you. In the end, the only lesson that took was that you can't depend on people. "I learned that men will disappear at the drop of a hat," Lindsay once said. "They don't care about their kids; they don't provide; they just disappear, and it's not that hard to make them go."

Mom perhaps sensed that Bob was regretting his decision to take on an additional child, because one day she called me into the living room to speak on the phone with Don Bowman, my biological father. It was a short but memorable conversation. He asked if I remembered wanting to have a farm with horses and cows and chickens, and I answered that I did. He asked if I remembered my siblings—Cory and Chelsea—and I did a little bit, so I said, "Kind of." He asked if I'd like to see him again.

I knew little about my biological father and barely recalled my life before Bob adopted me. I knew that Don had abandoned me because he didn't want to pay child support (or so Mom said). I knew that he was married to a woman named Cheryl, that he was tall, and that people thought I looked like him. And I knew that he was, in Mamaw's words, a "Holy Roller." That was the word she used for charismatic Christians who, she claimed, "handled snakes and screamed and wailed in church." This was enough to pique my curiosity: With little religious training, I was desperate for some exposure to a real church. I asked Mom if I could see him, and she agreed, so in the same summer that my legal father walked out of my life, my biological one walked back in. Mom had come full circle: Having cycled through a number of men in an effort to find me a father, she had settled on the original candidate.

Don Bowman had much more in common with Mom's side of the family than I expected. His father (and my grandfather), Don C. Bowman, also migrated from eastern Kentucky to southwest Ohio for work. After marrying and starting a family, my grandfather Bowman died suddenly, leaving behind two small children and a young wife. My grandmother remarried, and Dad spent much of his childhood in eastern Kentucky with his grandparents.

More than any other person, Dad understood what Kentucky meant to me, because it meant the same thing to him. His mom remarried early, and though her second husband was a good man, he was also very firm and an outsider—even the best stepparents take some getting used to. In Kentucky, among his people and with plenty of space, Dad could be himself. I felt the same way. There were two kinds of people: those whom I'd behave around because I wanted to impress them and those whom I'd behave around to avoid embarrassing myself. The latter people were out-siders, and Kentucky had none of them.

In many ways, Dad's life project was rebuilding for himself what he once had in Kentucky. When I first visited him, Dad had a modest house on a beautiful plot of land, fourteen acres in total. There was a medium-sized pond stocked with fish, a couple of fields for cows and horses, a barn, and a chicken coop. Every morning the kids would run to the chicken coop and grab the morning's haul of eggs—usually seven or eight, a perfect number for a family of five. During the day, we capered around the property with a dog in tow, caught frogs, and chased rabbits. It was exactly what Dad had done as a child, and exactly what I did with Mamaw in Kentucky.

I remember running through a field with Dad's collie, Dannie, a beautiful, bedraggled creature so gentle that he once caught a baby rabbit and carried it in his mouth, unharmed, to a human for inspection. I have no idea why I was running, but we both collapsed from exhaustion and lay in the grass, Dannie's head on my chest and my eyes staring at the blue sky. I don't know that I had ever felt so content, so completely unworried about life and its stresses.

Dad had built a home with an almost jarring serenity. He and his wife argued, but they rarely raised their voices at each other and never resorted to the brutal insults that were commonplace in Mom's house. None of their friends drank, not even socially. Even though they believed in corporal punishment, it was never doled out excessively or combined with verbal abuse—spanking was methodical and anger-free. My younger brother and sister clearly enjoyed their lives, even though they lacked pop music or R-rated movies.

What little I knew of Dad's character during his marriage to Mom came mostly secondhand. Mamaw, Aunt Wee, Lindsay, and Mom all told varying degrees of the same story: that Dad was mean. He yelled a lot and sometimes hit Mom. Lindsay told me that, as a child, I had a peculiarly large and misshapen head, and she attributed that to a time when she saw Dad push Mom aggressively.

Dad denies ever physically abusing anyone, including Mom. I suspect that they were physically abusive to each other in the way that Mom and most of her men were: a bit of pushing, some plate throwing, but nothing more. What I do know is that between the end of his marriage with Mom and the beginning of his marriage with Cheryl—which occurred when I was four—Dad had changed for the better. He credits a more serious involvement with his faith. In this, Dad embodied a phenomenon social scientists have observed for decades: Religious folks are much happier. Regular church attendees commit fewer crimes, are in better health, live longer, make more money, drop out of high school less frequently, and finish college more frequently than those who don't attend church at all.[16] MIT economist Jonathan Gruber even found that the relationship was *causal*: It's not just that people who happen to live successful lives also go to church, it's that church seems to promote good habits.

In his religious habits, Dad lived the stereotype of a culturally conservative Protestant with Southern roots, even though the stereotype is mostly inaccurate. Despite their reputation for clinging to their religion, the folks back home resembled Mamaw more than Dad: deeply religious but without any attachment to a real church community. Indeed, the only conservative Protestants I knew who attended church regularly were my dad and his family.[17] In the middle of the Bible Belt, active church attendance is actually quite low.[18]

Despite its reputation, Appalachia—especially northern Alabama and Georgia to southern Ohio—has far lower church attendance than the Midwest, parts of the Mountain West, and much of the space between Michigan and Montana. Oddly enough, we think we attend church more than we actually do. In a recent Gallup poll, Southerners and Midwesterners reported the highest rates of church attendance in the country. Yet *actual* church attendance is much lower in the South.

This pattern of deception has to do with cultural pressure. In southwestern Ohio, where I was born, both the Cincinnati and Dayton metropolitan regions have very low rates of church attendance, about the same as ultra-liberal San Francisco. No one I know in San Francisco would feel ashamed to admit that they don't go to church. (In fact, some of them might feel ashamed to admit that they do.) Ohio is the polar opposite. Even as a kid, I'd lie when people asked if I attended church regularly. According to Gallup, I wasn't alone in feeling that pressure.

The juxtaposition is jarring: Religious institutions remain a positive force in people's lives, but in a part of the country slammed by the decline of manufacturing, joblessness, addiction, and broken homes, church attendance has fallen off. Dad's church offered something desperately needed by people like me. For alcoholics, it gave them a community of support and a sense that they weren't fighting addiction alone. For expectant mothers, it offered a free home with job training and parenting classes. When someone needed a job, church friends could either provide one or make introductions. When Dad faced financial troubles, his church banded together and purchased a used car for the family. In the broken world I saw around me—and for the people struggling in that world—religion offered tangible assistance to keep the faithful on track.

Dad's faith attracted me even though I learned early on that it had played a significant role in the adoption that led to our long separation. While I really enjoyed the time we spent together, the pain of that adoption remained, and we spoke often of how and why it happened in the first place. For the first time, I heard his side of the story: that the adoption had nothing to do with a desire to avoid child support and that, far from simply "giving me away," as Mom and Mamaw had said, Dad had hired multiple lawyers and done everything within reason to keep me.

He worried that the custody war was destroying me. When I saw him during visitations before the adoption, I would hide under the bed for the first few hours, fearful that he would kidnap me and never let me see Mamaw again. Seeing his son in such a frightened state led him to reconsider his approach. Mamaw hated him, a fact I knew firsthand; but Dad said her hatred stemmed from the early days of his marriage to Mom, when he was far from a perfect husband. Sometimes when he came to pick me up, Mamaw would stand on the porch and stare at him, unblinking, clutching a hidden weapon. When he spoke to the court's child psychiatrist, he learned that I had begun acting out at school and was showing signs of emotional problems. (This I know to be true. After a few weeks in kindergarten, I was held back for a year. Two decades later, I ran into the teacher who had endured my first foray into kindergarten. She told me that I'd behaved so badly that she had nearly quit the profession—three weeks into her first year of teaching. That she remembered me twenty years later says a lot about my misbehavior.)

Eventually, Dad told me, he asked God for three signs that an adoption was in my best interest. Those signs apparently appeared, and I became the legal son of Bob, a man I'd known for barely a year. I don't doubt the truth of this account, and though I empathize with the obvious difficulty of the decision, I have never felt comfortable with the idea of leaving your child's fate to signs from God.

Yet this was a minor blip, all things considered. Just knowing that he had cared about me erased a lot of childhood pain. On balance, I loved my dad and his church. I'm not sure if I liked the structure or if I just wanted to share in something that was important to him—both, I suppose—but I became a devoted convert. I devoured books about young-earth creationism, and joined online chat rooms to challenge scientists on the theory of evolution. I learned about millennialist prophecy and convinced myself that the world would end in 2007. I even threw away my Black Sabbath CDs. Dad's church encouraged all of this because it doubted the wisdom of secular science and the morality of secular music.

Despite the lack of a legal relationship, I began spending a lot of time with Dad. I visited him on most holidays and spent every other weekend at his house. Though I loved seeing aunts, uncles, and cousins who hadn't been part of my life in years, the basic segregation of my two lives remained. Dad avoided Mom's side of the family, and vice versa. Lindsay and Mamaw appreciated Dad's new role in my life, but they continued to distrust him. To Mamaw, Dad was the "sperm donor" who had abandoned me at a critical juncture. Although I, too, resented Dad for the past, Mamaw's stubbornness didn't make things any easier.

Still, my relationship with Dad continued to develop, and so did my relationship with his church. The downside of his theology was that it promoted a certain segregation from the outside world. I couldn't listen to Eric Clapton at Dad's house—not because the lyrics were inappropriate but because Eric Clapton was influenced by demonic forces. I'd heard people joke that if you played Led Zeppelin's "Stairway to Heaven" backward, you'd hear some evil incantation, but a member of Dad's church spoke about the Zeppelin myth as if it were actually true.

These were quirks, and at first I understood them as little more than strict rules that I could either comply with or get around. Yet I was a curious kid, and the deeper I immersed myself in evangelical theology, the more I felt compelled to mistrust many sectors of society. Evolution and the Big Bang became ideologies to confront, not theories to understand. Many of the sermons I heard spent as much time criticizing other Christians as anything else. Theological battle lines were drawn, and those on the other side weren't just wrong about biblical interpretation, they were somehow unchristian. I admired my uncle Dan above all other men, but when he spoke of his Catholic acceptance of evolutionary theory, my admiration became tinged with suspicion. My new faith had put me on the lookout for heretics. Good friends who interpreted parts of the Bible differently were bad influences. Even Mamaw fell from favor because her religious views didn't conflict with her affinity for Bill Clinton.

As a young teenager thinking seriously for the first time about what I believed and why I believed it, I had an acute sense that the walls were closing in on "real" Christians. There was talk about the "war on Christmas"—which, as far as I could tell, consisted mainly of ACLU activists suing small towns for nativity displays. I read a book called *Persecution* by David Limbaugh about the various ways that Christians were discriminated against. The Internet was abuzz with talk of New York art displays that featured images of Christ or the Virgin Mary covered in feces. For the first time in my life, I felt like a persecuted minority.

All of this talk about Christians who weren't Christian enough, secularists indoctrinating our youth, art exhibits insulting our faith, and persecution by the elites made the world a scary and foreign place. Take gay rights, a particularly hot topic among conservative Protestants. I'll never forget the time I convinced myself that I was gay. I was eight or nine, maybe younger, and I stumbled upon a broadcast by some fire-and-brimstone preacher. The man spoke about the evils of homosexuals, how they had infiltrated our society, and how they were all destined for hell absent some serious repenting. At the time, the only thing I knew about gay men was that they preferred men to women. This described me perfectly: I disliked girls, and my best friend in the world was my buddy Bill. *Oh no, I'm going to hell.*

I broached this issue with Mamaw, confessing that I was gay and I was worried that I would burn in hell. She said, "Don't be a fucking idiot, how would you know that you're gay?" I explained my thought process. Mamaw chuckled and seemed to consider how she might explain to a boy my age. Finally she asked, "J.D., do you want to suck dicks?" I was flabbergasted. Why would someone want to do that? She repeated herself, and I said, "Of course not!" "Then," she said, "you're not gay. And even if you did want to suck dicks, that would be okay. God would still love you." That settled the matter. Apparently I didn't have to worry about being gay anymore. Now that I'm older, I recognize the profundity of her sentiment: Gay people, though unfamiliar, threatened nothing about Mamaw's being. There were more important things for a Christian to worry about.

In my new church, on the other hand, I heard more about the gay lobby and the war on Christmas than about any particular character trait that a Christian should aspire to have. I recalled that moment with Mamaw as an instance of secularist thinking rather than an act of Christian love. Morality was defined by not participating in this or that particular social malady: the gay agenda, evolutionary theory, Clintonian liberalism, or extramarital sex. Dad's church required so little of me. It was easy to be a Christian. The only affirmative teachings I remember drawing from church were that I shouldn't cheat on my wife and that I shouldn't be afraid to preach the gospel to others. So I planned a life of monogamy and tried to convert other people, even my seventh-grade science teacher, who was Muslim.

The world lurched toward moral corruption—slouching toward Gomorrah. The Rapture was coming, we thought. Apocalyptic imagery filled the weekly sermons and the *Left Behind* books (one of the best-selling fiction series of all time, which I devoured). Folks would discuss whether the Antichrist was already alive and, if so, which world leader it might be. Someone told me that he expected I'd marry a very pretty girl if the Lord hadn't come by the time I reached marrying age. The End Times were the natural finish for a culture sliding so quickly toward the abyss.

Other authors have noted the terrible retention rates of evangelical churches and blamed precisely that sort of theology for their decline.[19] I didn't appreciate it as a kid. Nor did I realize that the religious views I developed during my early years with Dad were sowing the seeds for an outright rejection of the Christian faith. What I did know is that, despite its downsides, I loved both my new church and the man who introduced me to it. The timing, it turned out, was impeccable: The next months would bring a desperate need for both a heavenly father and an earthly one.

Chapter 7

In the fall after I turned thirteen, Mom began dating Matt, a younger guy who worked as a firefighter. I adored Matt from the start—he was my favorite of all of Mom's men, and we still keep in touch. One night I was at home watching TV, waiting for Mom to get home from work with a bucket of KFC for dinner. I had two responsibilities that evening: first, track down Lindsay in case she was hungry; and second, run food over to Mamaw as soon as Mom arrived. Shortly before I expected Mom, Mamaw called. "Where is your mother?"

"I don't know. What's wrong, Mamaw?"

Her response, more than anything I've ever heard, is seared in my memory. She was worried—scared, even. The hillbilly accent that she usually hid dripped from her lips. *"No one has seen or heard from Papaw."* I told her I'd call as soon as Mom got home, which I expected would happen soon.

I figured Mamaw was overreacting. But then I considered the utter predictability of Papaw's schedule. He woke at six in the morning every day, without an alarm clock, then drove to McDonald's at seven to grab a coffee with his old Armco buddies.

After a couple of hours of conversation, he would amble over to Mamaw's house and spend the morning watching TV or playing cards. If he left at all before dinnertime, he might briefly visit his friend Paul's hardware store. Without exception, he stayed at Mamaw's house to greet me when I came home from school. And if I didn't go to Mamaw's—if I went to Mom's, as I did when times were good—he'd usually come over and say goodbye before he went home for the evening. That he had missed all of these events meant that something was very wrong.

Mom walked in the door a few minutes after Mamaw called, and I was already sobbing. "Papaw . . . Papaw, I think he's dead." The rest is a blur: I think I relayed Mamaw's message; we picked her up down the street and sped over to Papaw's house, no more than a few minutes' drive away. I knocked on his door violently. Mom ran to the back door, screamed, and came around front, both to tell Mamaw that he was hunched over in his chair and to grab a rock. She then broke and went in through a window, unlocked and opened the door, and tended to her father. By then he had been dead for nearly a day.

Mom and Mamaw sobbed uncontrollably as we waited for an ambulance. I tried to hug Mamaw, but she was beside herself and unresponsive even to me. When she stopped crying, she clutched me to her chest and told me to go say goodbye before they took his body away. I tried, but the medical technician kneeling beside him gazed at me as if she thought I was creepy for wanting to look at a dead body. I didn't tell her the real reason I had walked back to my slouching Papaw.

After the ambulance took Papaw's body away, we drove immediately to Aunt Wee's house. I guessed Mom had called her, because she descended from her porch with tears in her eyes.

We all hugged her before squeezing into the car and heading back to Mamaw's. The adults gave me the unenviable task of tracking down Lindsay and giving her the news. This was before cell phones, and Lindsay, being a seventeen-year-old, was difficult to reach. She wasn't answering the house phone, and none of her friends answered my calls. Mamaw's house sat literally five houses away from Mom's—313 McKinley to 303—so I listened to the adults make plans and watched out the window for signs of my sister's return. The adults spoke about funeral arrangements, where Papaw would want to be buried—"In Jackson, goddammit," Mamaw insisted—and who would call Uncle Jimmy and tell him to come home.

Lindsay returned home shortly before midnight. I trudged down the street and opened our door. She was walking down the stairs but stopped cold when she saw my face, red and blotchy from crying all day. "Papaw," I blurted out. "He's dead." Lindsay collapsed on the stairs, and I ran up and embraced her. We sat there for a few minutes, crying as two children do when they find out that the most important man in their lives has died. Lindsay said something then, and though I don't remember the exact phrase, I do remember that Papaw had just done some work on her car, and she was muttering something through the tears about taking advantage of him.

Lindsay was a teenager when Papaw died, at the height of that weird mixture of thinking you know everything and caring too much about how others perceive you. Papaw was many things, but he was never cool. He wore the same old T-shirt every day with a front pocket just big enough to fit a pack of cigarettes. He always smelled of mildew, because he washed his clothes but let them dry "naturally," meaning packed together in a washing machine. A lifetime of smoking had blessed him with an unlimited supply of phlegm, and he had no problem sharing that phlegm with everyone, no matter the time or occasion. He listened to Johnny Cash on perpetual repeat and drove an old El Camino—a car truck—everywhere he went. In other words, Papaw wasn't ideal company for a beautiful seventeen-year-old girl with an active social life. Thus, she took advantage of him in the same way that every young girl takes advantage of a father: She loved and admired him, she asked him for things that he sometimes gave her, and she didn't pay him a lot of attention when she was around her friends.

To this day, being able to "take advantage" of someone is the measure in my mind of having a parent. For me and Lindsay, the fear of imposing stalked our minds, infecting even the food we ate. We recognized instinctively that many of the people we depended on weren't supposed to play that role in our lives, so much so that it was one of the first things Lindsay thought of when she learned of Papaw's death. We were conditioned to feel that we couldn't really depend on people—that, even as children, asking someone for a meal or for help with a broken-down automobile was a luxury that we shouldn't indulge in too much lest we fully tap the reservoir of goodwill serving as a safety valve in our lives. Mamaw and Papaw did everything they could to fight that instinct. On our rare trips to a nice restaurant, they would interrogate me about what I truly wanted until I'd confess that yes, I did want the steak. And then they'd order it for me over my protests. No matter how imposing, no figure could erase that feeling entirely. Papaw had come the closest, but he clearly hadn't succeeded all the way, and now he was gone.

Papaw died on a Tuesday, and I know this because when Mom's boyfriend, Matt, drove me to a local diner the next morning to pick up food for the whole family, the Lynyrd Skynyrd song "Tuesday's Gone" was playing on the radio. "But somehow I've got to carry on / Tuesday's gone with the wind." That was the moment it really hit me that Papaw was never coming back. The adults did what people do when a loved one dies: They planned a funeral, figured out how to pay for it, and hoped that they did the deceased some justice. We hosted a visitation in Middletown that Thursday so all the locals could pay their respects, then had a second visitation in Jackson on Friday before a Saturday funeral. Even in death, Papaw had one foot in Ohio and another in the holler.

Everyone I cared to see came to the funeral in Jackson—Uncle Jimmy and his kids, our extended family and friends, and all of the Blanton men who were still kicking. It occurred to me as I saw these titans of my family that, for the first eleven or so years of my life, I saw them during happy times—family reunions and holidays or lazy summers and long weekends—and in the two most recent years I'd seen them only at funerals.

At Papaw's funeral, as at other hillbilly funerals I've witnessed, the preacher invited everyone to stand up and say a few words about the deceased. As I sat next to Uncle Jimmy in the pew, I sobbed throughout the hour-long funeral, my eyes so irritated by the end that I could hardly see. Still, I knew this was it, and that if I didn't stand up and speak my piece, I'd regret it for the rest of my life.

I thought about a moment nearly a decade earlier that I'd heard about but didn't remember. I was four or five, sitting in a church pew for a great-uncle's funeral in that same Deaton funeral home in Jackson. We had just arrived after a long drive from Middletown, and when the minister asked us to bow our heads and pray, I bowed my head and passed out. Mamaw's older brother Uncle Pet lay me on my side with a Bible as a pillow and thought nothing more of it. I was asleep for what happened next, but I've heard some version of it a hundred times. Even today, when I see someone who attended that funeral, they tell me about my hillbilly Mamaw and Papaw.

When I failed to appear in the crowd of mourners leaving the church, Mamaw and Papaw grew suspicious. There were perverts even in Jackson, they told me, who wanted to stick sticks up your butt and "blow on your pecker" as much as the perverts in Ohio or Indiana or California. Papaw hatched a plan: There were only two exits to Deaton's, and no one had driven away yet. Papaw ran to the car and grabbed a .44 Magnum for himself and a .38 Special for Mamaw. They manned the exits to the funeral home and checked every car. When they encountered an old friend, they explained the situation and enlisted help. When they met someone else, they searched the cars like goddamned DEA agents.

Uncle Pet approached, frustrated that Mamaw and Papaw were holding up traffic. When they explained, Pet howled with laughter: "He's asleep in the church pew, let me show you." After they found me, they allowed traffic to flow freely once again.

I thought about Papaw buying me a BB gun with a mounted scope. He placed the gun on his workbench with a vise to hold it in place and fired repeatedly at a target. After each shot, we adjusted the scope, aligning the crosshairs with where the BB impacted the target. And then he taught me how to shoot—how to focus on the sights and not the target, how to exhale before pulling the trigger. Years later, our marine boot camp marksmanship instructors would tell us that the kids who already "knew" how to shoot performed the worst, because they'd learned improper fundamentals. That was true with one exception: me. From Papaw, I had learned excellent fundamentals, and I qualified with an M16 rifle as an expert, the highest category, with one of the highest scores in my entire platoon.

Papaw was gruff to the point of absurdity. To every suggestion or behavior he didn't like, Papaw had one reply: "Bullshit." That was everyone's cue to shut the hell up. His hobby was cars: He loved buying, trading, and fixing them. One day not long after Papaw quit drinking, Uncle Jimmy came home to find him fixing an old automobile on the street. "He was cussing up a storm. 'These goddamned Japanese cars, cheap pieces of shit. What a stupid motherfucker who made this part.' I just listened to him, not knowing a single person was around, and he just kept carrying on and complaining. I thought he sounded miserable." Uncle Jimmy had recently started working and was eager to spend his money to help his dad out. So he offered to take the car to a shop and get it fixed. The suggestion caught Papaw completely off guard. "What? Why?" he asked innocently. "I love fixing cars."

Papaw had a beer belly and a chubby face but skinny arms and legs. He never apologized with words. While helping Aunt Wee move across the country, she admonished him for his earlier alcoholism and asked why they rarely had the chance to talk. "Well, talk now. We've got all fucking day in the car together." But he did apologize with deeds: The rare times when he lost his temper with me were always followed with a new toy or a trip to the ice cream parlor.

Papaw was a terrifying hillbilly made for a different time and place. During that cross-country drive with Aunt Wee, they stopped at a highway rest stop in the early morning. Aunt Wee decided to comb her hair and brush her teeth and thus spent more time in the ladies' room than Papaw thought reasonable. He kicked open the door holding a loaded revolver, like a character in a Liam Neeson movie. He was sure, he explained, that she was being raped by some pervert. Years later, after Aunt Wee's dog growled at her infant baby, Papaw told her husband, Dan, that unless he got rid of the dog, Papaw would feed it a steak marinated in antifreeze. He wasn't joking: Three decades earlier, he had made the same promise to a neighbor after a dog nearly bit my mom. A week later that dog was dead. In that funeral home I thought about these things, too.

Most of all I thought about Papaw and me. I thought about the hours we spent practicing increasingly complex math problems. He taught me that lack of knowledge and lack of intelligence were not the same. The former could be remedied with a little patience and a lot of hard work. And the latter? "Well, I guess you're up shit creek without a paddle."

I thought about how Papaw would get on the ground with me and Aunt Wee's baby girls and play with us like a child. Despite his "bullshits" and his grouchiness, he never met a hug or a kiss that he didn't welcome. He bought Lindsay a crappy car and fixed it up, and after she wrecked it, he bought her another one and fixed that one up, too, just so she didn't feel like she "came from nothing." I thought about losing my temper with Mom or Lindsay or Mamaw, and how those were among the few times Papaw ever showed a mean streak, because, as he once told me, "the measure of a man is how he treats the women in his family." His wisdom came from experience, from his own earlier failures with treating the women in his family well.

I stood up in that funeral home, resolved to tell everyone just how important he was. "I never had a dad," I explained. "But Papaw was always there for me, and he taught me the things that men needed to know." Then I spoke the sum of his influence on my life: "He was the best dad that anyone could ever ask for."

After the funeral, a number of people told me that they appreciated my bravery and courage. Mom was not among them, which struck me as odd. When I located her in the crowd, she seemed trapped in some sort of trance: saying little, even to those who approached her; her movements slow and her body slouched.

Mamaw, too, seemed out of sorts. Kentucky was usually the one place where she was completely in her element. In Middletown, she could never truly be herself. At Perkins, our favorite breakfast spot, Mamaw's mouth would sometimes earn a request from the manager that she keep her voice down or watch her language. "That fucker," she'd mutter under her breath, chastened and uncomfortable. But at Bill's Family Diner, the only restaurant in Jackson worth sitting down at for a meal, she'd scream at the kitchen staff to "hurry the hell up" and they'd laugh and say, "Okay, Bonnie." Then she'd look at me and tell me, "You know I'm just fucking with them, right? They know I'm not a mean old bitch."

In Jackson, among old friends and real hillbillies, she needed no filter. At her brother's funeral a few years earlier, Mamaw and her niece Denise convinced themselves that one of the pallbearers was a pervert, so they broke into his funeral home office and searched through his belongings. They found an extensive magazine collection, including a few issues of *Beaver Hunt* (a periodical that I can assure you has nothing to do with aquatic mammals). Mamaw found it hilarious. "Fucking *Beaver Hunt*!" she'd roar.

"Who comes up with this shit?" She and Denise hatched a plot to take the magazines home and mail them to the pallbearer's wife. After a short deliberation, she changed her mind. "With my luck," she told me, "we'll get in a crash on the way back to Ohio and the police will find these damned things in my trunk. I'll be damned if I'm going to go out with everyone thinking I was a lesbian—and a perverted one at that!" So they threw the magazines away to "teach that pervert a lesson" and never spoke of it again. This side of Mamaw rarely showed itself outside of Jackson.

Deaton's funeral home in Jackson—where she'd stolen those *Beaver Hunts*—was organized like a church. In the center of the building was a main sanctuary flanked by larger rooms with couches and tables. On the other two sides were hallways with exits to a few smaller rooms—offices for staff, a tiny kitchen, and bathrooms. I've spent much of my life in that tiny funeral home, saying goodbye to aunts and uncles and cousins and great-grandparents. And whether she went to Deaton's to bury an old friend, a brother, or her beloved mother, Mamaw greeted every guest, laughed loudly, and cursed proudly.

So it was a surprise to me when, during Papaw's visitation, I went searching for comfort and found Mamaw alone in a corner of the funeral home, recharging batteries that I never knew could go empty. She stared blankly at the floor, her fire replaced with something unfamiliar. I knelt before her and laid my head in her lap and said nothing. At that moment, I realized that Mamaw was not invincible.

In hindsight, it's clear that there was more than grief to both Mamaw's and Mom's behavior. Lindsay, Matt, and Mamaw did their best to hide it from me. Mamaw forbade me to stay at

Mom's, under the ruse that Mamaw needed me with her as she grieved. Perhaps they hoped to give me a little space to mourn Papaw. I don't know.

I didn't see at first that something had veered off course. Papaw was dead, and everyone processed it differently. Lindsay spent a lot of time with her friends and was always on the move. I stayed as close to Mamaw as possible and read the Bible a lot. Mom slept more than usual, and I figured this was her way of coping. At home, she lacked even a modicum of temper control. Lindsay failed to do the dishes properly, or forgot to take out the dog, and Mom's anger poured out: "My dad was the only one who really understood me!" she'd scream. "I've lost him, and you're not making this any easier!" Mom had always had a temper, though, so I dismissed even this.

Mom seemed bothered that anyone but her was grieving. Aunt Wee's grief was unjustified, because Mom and Papaw had a special bond. So, too, was Mamaw's, for she didn't even like Papaw and chose not to live under the same roof. Lindsay and I needed to get over ourselves, for it was Mom's father, not ours, who had just died. The first indication that our lives were about to change came one morning when I woke and strolled over to Mom's house, where I knew Lindsay and Mom were sleeping. I went first to Lindsay's room, but she was asleep in my room instead. I knelt beside her, woke her up, and she hugged me tightly. After a little while, she said earnestly, "We'll get through this, J."—that was her nickname for me—"I promise." I still have no idea why she slept in my room that night, but I would soon learn what she promised we'd get through.

A few days after the funeral, I walked onto Mamaw's front porch, looked down the street, and saw an incredible commotion.

Mom was standing in a bath towel in her front yard, screaming at the only people who truly loved her: to Matt, "You're a fucking loser nobody"; to Lindsay, "You're a selfish bitch, he was my dad, not yours, so stop acting like you just lost your father"; to Tammy, her unbelievably kind friend who was secretly gay, "The only reason you act like my friend is because you want to fuck me." I ran over and begged Mom to calm down, but by then a police cruiser was already on the scene. I arrived on the front porch as a police officer grabbed Mom's shoulders and she collapsed on the ground, struggling and kicking. Then the officer grabbed Mom and carried her to the cruiser, and she fought the whole way. There was blood on the porch, and someone said that she had tried to cut her wrists. I don't think the officer arrested her, though I don't know what happened. Mamaw arrived on the scene and took Lindsay and me with her. I remember thinking that if Papaw were here, he would know what to do.

Papaw's death cast light upon something that had previously lurked in the shadows. Only a kid could have missed the writing on the wall, I suppose. A year earlier, Mom had lost her job at Middletown Hospital after Rollerblading through the emergency room. At the time I saw Mom's bizarre behavior as the consequence of her divorce from Bob. Similarly, Mamaw's occasional references to Mom "getting loaded" seemed like random comments of a woman known for her willingness to say anything, not a diagnosis of a deteriorating reality. Not long after Mom lost her job, during my trip to California, I heard from her just once. I had no idea that, behind the scenes, the adults—meaning Mamaw on the one hand and Uncle Jimmy and his wife, Aunt Donna, on the other—were debating whether I should move permanently to California.

Mom flailing and screaming in the street was the culmination of the things I hadn't seen. She'd begun taking prescription narcotics not long after we moved to Preble County. I believe the problem started with a legitimate prescription, but soon enough, Mom was stealing from her patients and getting so high that turning an emergency room into a skating rink seemed like a good idea. Papaw's death turned a semi-functioning addict into a woman unable to follow the basic norms of adult behavior.

In this way, Papaw's death permanently altered the trajectory of our family. Before his death, I had settled into the chaotic but happy routine of splitting time between Mom's and Mamaw's. Boyfriends came and went, Mom had good days and bad, but I always had an escape route. With Papaw gone and Mom in rehab at the Cincinnati Center for Addiction Treatment—or "the CAT house," as we called it—I began to feel myself a burden. Though she never said anything to make me feel unwanted, Mamaw's life had been a constant struggle: From the poverty of the holler to Papaw's abuse, from Aunt Wee's teenage marriage to Mom's rap sheet, Mamaw had spent the better part of her seven decades managing crises. And now, when most people her age were enjoying the fruits of retirement, she was raising two teenage grandchildren. Without Papaw to help her, that burden seemed twice as heavy. In the months after Papaw's death, I remembered the woman I found in an isolated corner of Deaton's funeral home and couldn't shake the feeling that, no matter what aura of strength Mamaw projected, that other woman lived somewhere inside her.

So instead of retreating to Mamaw's house, or calling her every time problems arose with Mom, I relied on Lindsay and on myself. Lindsay was a recent high school graduate, and I had just started seventh grade, but we made it work. Sometimes

Matt or Tammy brought us food, but we largely fended for ourselves: Hamburger Helper, TV dinners, Pop-Tarts, and breakfast cereal. I'm not sure who paid the bills (probably Mamaw). We didn't have a lot of structure—Lindsay once came home from work to find me hanging out with a couple of her friends, all of us drunk—but in some ways we didn't need it. When Lindsay learned that I got the beer from a friend of hers, she didn't lose her cool or laugh at the indulgence; she kicked everyone out and then lectured me on substance abuse.

We saw Mamaw often, and she asked about us constantly. But we both enjoyed the independence, and I think we enjoyed the feeling that we burdened no one except perhaps each other. Lindsay and I had grown so good at managing crises, so emotionally stoic even as the very planet seemed to lose its cool, that taking care of ourselves seemed easy. No matter how much we loved Mom, our lives were easier with one less person to care for.

Did we struggle? Certainly. We received one letter from the school district informing us that I had collected so many unexcused absences that my parents might be summoned before the school or even prosecuted by the city. We found this letter hilarious: One of my parents had already faced a prosecution of sorts and hardly possessed any walking-around liberty, while the other was sufficiently off the grid that "summoning" him would require some serious detective work. We also found it frightening: Without a legal guardian around to sign the letter, we didn't know what the hell to do. But as we had with other challenges, we improvised. Lindsay forged Mom's signature, and the school district stopped sending letters home.

On designated weekdays and weekends, we visited our mother at the CAT house. Between the hills of Kentucky, Mamaw and her guns, and Mom's outbursts, I thought that I had seen it all. But Mom's newest problem exposed me to the underworld of American addiction. Wednesdays were always dedicated to a group activity—some type of training for the family. All of the addicts and their families sat in a large room with each family assigned to an individual table, engaged in some discussion meant to teach us about addiction and its triggers. In one session, Mom explained that she used drugs to escape the stress of paying bills and to dull the pain of Papaw's death. In another, Lindsay and I learned that standard sibling conflict made it more difficult for Mom to resist temptation.

These sessions provoked little more than arguments and raw emotion, which I suppose was their purpose. On the nights when we sat in that giant hall with other families—all of whom were either black or Southern-accented whites like us—we heard screaming and fighting, children telling their parents that they hated them, sobbing parents begging forgiveness in one breath and then blaming their families in the next. It was there that I first heard Lindsay tell Mom how she resented having to play the caretaker in the wake of Papaw's death instead of grieving for him, how she hated watching me grow attached to some boyfriend of Mom's only to see him walk out on us. Perhaps it was the setting, or perhaps it was the fact that Lindsay was almost eighteen, but as my sister confronted my mother, I began to see my sister as the real adult. And our routine at home only enhanced her stature.

Mom's rehab proceeded apace, and her condition apparently improved with time. Sundays were designated as unstructured family time: We couldn't take Mom off-site, but we were able to eat and watch TV and talk as normal. Sundays were usually happy, though Mom did angrily chide us during one visit because our relationship with Mamaw had grown too close. "I'm your mother, not her," she told us. I realized that Mom had begun to regret the seeds she'd sown with Lindsay and me.

When Mom came home a few months later, she brought a new vocabulary along with her. She regularly recited the Serenity Prayer, a staple of addiction circles in which the faithful ask God for the "serenity to accept the things [they] cannot change." Drug addiction was a disease, and just as I wouldn't judge a cancer patient for a tumor, so I shouldn't judge a narcotics addict for her behavior. At thirteen, I found this patently absurd, and Mom and I often argued over whether her newfound wisdom was scientific truth or an excuse for people whose decisions destroyed a family. Oddly enough, it's probably both: Research does reveal a genetic disposition to substance abuse, but those who believe their addiction is a disease show less of an inclination to resist it. Mom was telling herself the truth, but the truth was not setting her free.

I didn't believe in any of the slogans or sentiments, but I did believe she was trying. Addiction treatment seemed to give Mom a sense of purpose, and it gave us something to bond over. I read what I could on her "disease" and even made a habit of attending some of her Narcotics Anonymous meetings, which proceeded precisely as you'd expect: a depressing conference room, a dozen or so chairs, and a bunch of strangers sitting in a circle, introducing themselves as "Bob, and I'm an addict." I thought that if I participated, she might actually get better.

At one meeting a man walked in a few minutes late, smelling like a garbage can. His matted hair and dirty clothes evidenced a life on the streets, a truth he confirmed as soon as he opened his mouth. "My kids won't speak to me; no one will," he told us. "I scrounge together what money I can and spend it on smack. To-night I couldn't find any money or any smack, so I came in here because it looked warm." The organizer asked if he'd be willing to try giving up the drugs for more than one night, and the man answered with admirable candor: "I could say yes, but honestly, probably not. I'll probably be back at it tomorrow night."

I never saw that man again. Before he left, someone did ask him where he was from. "Well, I've lived here in Hamilton for most of my life. But I was born down in eastern Kentucky, Owsley County." At the time, I didn't know enough about Kentucky geography to tell the man that he had been born no more than twenty miles from my grandparents' childhood home.

Chapter 8

By the time I finished eighth grade, Mom had been sober for at least a year, and she'd been dating Matt for two or three years. I was doing well in school, and Mamaw had taken a couple vacations—one trip to California to visit Uncle Jimmy and another to Las Vegas with her friend Kathy. Lindsay had married soon after Papaw's death. I loved her husband, Kevin, and still do, for a simple reason: He never mistreated her. That's all I ever wanted in a mate for my sister. Just under a year after their wedding, Lindsay gave birth to her son, Kameron. She was a mom, and a damn good one at that. I was proud of her, and I adored my new nephew. Aunt Wee also had two small children, which gave me three little kids to dote on. I saw all of this as a sign of family renewal. The summer before high school was thus a hopeful one.

That same summer, however, Mom announced that I'd be moving in with Matt in his Dayton home. I liked Matt, and by then Mom had lived in Dayton with him for a little while. But Dayton was a forty-five-minute drive from Mamaw's, and Mom made it clear that she wanted me to attend school in Dayton. I liked my life in Middletown—I wanted to attend the high school, I loved my friends, and although it was a bit unconventional, I enjoyed splitting time between Mom's and Mamaw's houses during the week and hanging out with Dad on the weekends. Importantly, I could always go to Mamaw's house if I needed to, and that made all the difference. I remembered life when I didn't have that safety valve, and I didn't want to go back to those days. Moreover, any move would be without Lindsay and Kameron. So when Mom made her announcement about moving in with Matt, I belted out, "Absolutely not," and stormed away.

Mom drew from this conversation that I had anger problems and scheduled a time for me to meet with her therapist. I didn't know she had a therapist or the money to afford one, but I agreed to meet with this lady. Our first meeting took place the following week in a musty old office near Dayton, Ohio, where a nondescript middle-aged woman, Mom, and I tried to understand why I was so angry. I recognized that human beings aren't very good at judging themselves: I may have been wrong that I was no angrier (in fact, considerably less so) than most of the people in my life. Maybe Mom was right and I did have some anger problems. I tried to keep an open mind. If nothing else, I thought, this woman might give Mom and me an opportunity to get everything in the open.

But that first session felt like an ambush. Immediately, the woman began asking why I would scream at my mother and storm off, why I didn't recognize that she was my mother and that I had to live with her by law. The therapist chronicled "outbursts" that I'd allegedly had, some going back to a time I couldn't remember—the time I threw a tantrum in a department store as a five-year-old, my fight with another child in school (the school bully, whom I didn't want to punch but did so at Mamaw's encouragement), the times I'd run from home to my grandparents' house because of Mom's "discipline." Clearly this woman had developed an impression of me based solely on what Mom had told her. If I didn't have an anger problem before, I did now.

"Do you have any idea what you're talking about?" I asked. At fourteen, I knew at least a little about professional ethics. "Aren't you supposed to ask me what I think about things and not just criticize me?" I launched into an hour-long summary of my life to that point. I didn't tell the whole story, since I knew I had to choose my words carefully: During Mom's domestic violence case a couple of years earlier, Lindsay and I had let slip some unsavory details about Mom's parenting, and because it counted as a new revelation of abuse, the family counselor was required to report it to child services. So I didn't miss the irony of lying to a therapist (to protect Mom) lest I ignite another intervention by the county children's services. I explained the situation well enough: After an hour, she said simply, "Perhaps we should meet alone."

I saw this woman as an obstacle to overcome—an obstacle placed by Mom—not as someone who might help. I explained only half of my feelings: that I had no interest in putting a forty-five-minute barrier between me and everyone I had ever de-pended on so I could replant myself with a man I knew would be sent packing. The therapist obviously understood. What I didn't tell her is that for the first time in my life, I felt trapped. There was no Papaw, and Mamaw—a longtime smoker with the em-physema to prove it—seemed too frail and exhausted to care for a fourteen-year-old boy. My aunt and uncle had two young kids. Lindsay was newly married and had a child of her own. I had nowhere to go. I'd seen chaos and fighting, violence, drugs, and a great deal of instability. But I'd never felt like I had no way out. When the therapist asked me what I'd do, I replied that I would probably go live with my dad. She said that this sounded like a good idea. When I walked out of her office, I thanked her for her time and knew that I'd never see her again.

Mom had a massive blind spot in the way that she perceived the world. That she would ask me to move with her to Dayton, that she seemed genuinely surprised by my resistance, and that she would subject me to such a one-sided introduction to a therapist meant that Mom didn't understand something about the way that Lindsay and I ticked. Lindsay once told me, "Mom just doesn't get it." I initially disagreed with her: "Of course she gets it; it's just the way she is, something she can't change." After the incident with the therapist, I knew that Lindsay was right.

Mamaw was unhappy when I told her that I planned to live with Dad, and so was everyone else. No one really understood it, and I felt unable to say much about it. I knew that if I told the truth, I'd have a few people offering their spare bedrooms, and all of them would submit to Mamaw's demand that I live permanently with her. I also knew that living with Mamaw came with a lot of guilt, and a lot of questions about why I didn't live with my mom or dad, and a lot of whispers from a lot of people to Mamaw that she just needed to take a break and enjoy her golden years. That feeling of being a burden to Mamaw wasn't something I imagined; it came from a number of small cues, from the things she muttered under her breath, and from the weariness she wore like a dark piece of clothing. I didn't want that, so I chose what seemed like the least bad option.

In some ways, I loved living with Dad. His life was *normal* in precisely the way I'd always wanted mine to be. My stepmom worked part-time but was usually home. Dad came home from work around the same time each day. One of them (usually my stepmom but sometimes Dad) made dinner every night, which we ate as a family. Before each meal, we'd say grace (something I'd always liked but had never done outside of Kentucky). On weeknights, we'd watch some family sitcom together. And Dad and Cheryl never screamed at each other. Once, I heard them raise their voices during an argument about money, but slightly elevated volumes were far different from screaming.

On my first weekend at Dad's house—the first weekend I had ever spent with him when I knew that, come Monday, I wouldn't be going somewhere else—my younger brother invited a friend to sleep over. We fished in Dad's pond, fed horses, and grilled steaks for dinner. That night, we watched *Indiana Jones* movies until the early-morning hours. There was no fighting, no adults hurling insults at one another, no glass china shattering angrily against the wall or floor. It was a boring evening. And it epitomized what attracted me to Dad's home.

What I never lost, though, was the sense of being on guard. When I moved in with my father, I'd known him for two years. I knew that he was a good man, a little quiet, a devout Christian from a very strict religious tradition. When we first reconnected, he made it clear that he didn't care for my taste in classic rock, especially Led Zeppelin. He wasn't mean about it—that wasn't his style—and he didn't tell me I couldn't listen to my favorite bands; he just advised that I listen to Christian rock instead. I could never tell my dad that I played a nerdy collectible card game called Magic, because I feared he'd think the cards were satanic—after all, kids at the church youth group often spoke of Magic and its evil influence on young Christians. And as most teenagers do, I had so many questions about my faith—whether it was compatible with modern science, for instance, or whether this or that denomination was correct on particular doctrinal disputes.

I doubt he would have gotten upset if I'd asked those questions, but I never did because I didn't know how he'd respond. I didn't know whether he'd tell me I was a spawn of Satan and send me away. I didn't know how much of our new relationship was built on his sense that I was a good kid. I didn't know how he'd react if I listened to those Zeppelin CDs in his house with my younger siblings around. That not knowing gnawed at me to the point where I could no longer take it.

I think Mamaw understood what was going on in my head, even though I never told her explicitly. We spoke on the phone frequently, and one night she told me that I had to know she loved me more than anything and she wanted me to return home when I was ready. "This is your home, J.D., and always will be." The next day, I called Lindsay and asked her to come and get me. She had a job, a house, a husband, and a baby. But she said, "I'll be there in forty-five minutes." I apologized to Dad, who was heartbroken by my decision. But he understood: "You can't stay away from that crazy grandma of yours. I know she's good to you." It was a stunning admission from a man to whom Mamaw never said a nice word. And it was the first indication that Dad understood the complex and conflicting feelings I'd developed. That meant a great deal to me. When Lindsay and her family came to get me, I got in the car, sighed, and said to her, "Thanks for taking me home." I gave my infant nephew a kiss on the forehead and said nothing else until we got to Mamaw's.

I spent the rest of the summer mostly with Mamaw. A few weeks with Dad had given me no epiphanies: I still felt caught between a desire to stay with her and a fear that my presence was depriving her of the comforts of old age. So before my freshman year started, I told Mom that I'd live with her so long as I could stay in Middletown's schools and see Mamaw whenever I wanted. She said something about needing to transfer to a Dayton school after my freshman year, but I figured we'd cross that bridge in a year, when we had to.

Living with Mom and Matt was like having a front-row seat to the end of the world. The fighting was relatively normal by my standards (and Mom's), but I'm sure poor Matt kept asking himself how and when he'd hopped the express train to crazy town. It was just the three of us in that house, and it was clear to all that it wouldn't work out. It was only a matter of time. Matt was a nice guy, and as Lindsay and I joked, nice guys never survived their encounters with our family.

Given the state of Mom and Matt's relationship, I was surprised when I came home from school one day early during my sophomore year and Mom announced that she was getting married. Perhaps, I thought, things weren't quite as bad as I expected. "I honestly thought you and Matt were going to break up," I said. "You fight every day." "Well," she replied, "I'm not getting married to him."

It was a story that even I found incredible. Mom had been working as a nurse at a local dialysis center, a job she'd held for a few months. Her boss, about ten years her senior, asked her out to dinner one night. She obliged, and with her relationship in shambles, she agreed to marry him a week later. She told me on a Thursday. On Saturday we moved into Ken's house. His home was my fourth in two years.

Ken was born in Korea but raised by an American veteran and his wife. During that first week in his house, I decided to inspect his small greenhouse and stumbled upon a relatively mature marijuana plant. I told Mom, who told Ken, and by the end of the day it had been replaced with a tomato plant. When I confronted Ken, he stammered a bit and finally said, "It's for medicinal purposes, don't worry about it."

Ken's three children—a young girl and two boys about the same age I was—found the new arrangement as strange as I did. The oldest boy fought constantly with Mom, which—thanks to the Appalachian honor code—meant that he fought constantly with me. Shortly before I went to bed one night, I came downstairs just as he called her a bitch. No self-respecting hillbilly could stand idly by, so I made it abundantly clear that I meant to beat my new stepbrother to within an inch of his life. So unquenchable was my appetite for violence that night that Mom and Ken decided that my new stepbrother and I should be separated. I wasn't even particularly angry. My desire to fight arose more out of a sense of duty. But it was a strong sense of duty, so Mom and I went to Mamaw's for the night.

I remember watching an episode of *The West Wing* about education in America, which the majority of people rightfully believe is the key to opportunity. In it, the fictional president debates whether he should push school vouchers (giving public money to schoolchildren so that they escape failing public schools) or instead focus exclusively on fixing those same failing schools. That debate is important, of course—for a long time, much of my failing school district qualified for vouchers—but it was striking that in an entire discussion about why poor kids struggled in school, the emphasis rested entirely on public institutions. As a teacher at my old high school told me recently, "They want us to be shepherds to these kids. But no one wants to talk about the fact that many of them are raised by wolves."

I don't know what happened the day after Mom and I escaped Ken's to Mamaw's for the night. Maybe I had a test that I wasn't able to study for. Maybe I had a homework assignment due that I never had the time to complete. What I do know is that I was a sophomore in high school, and I was miserable. The constant moving and fighting, the seemingly endless carousel of new people I had to meet, learn to love, and then forget—this, and not my subpar public school, was the real barrier to opportunity.

I didn't know it, but I was close to the precipice. I had nearly failed out of my freshmen year of high school, earning a 2.1 GPA. I didn't do my homework, I didn't study, and my attendance was abysmal. Some days I'd fake an illness, and others I'd just refuse to go. When I did go, I did so only to avoid a repeat of the letters the school had sent home a few years earlier—the ones that said if I didn't go to school, the administration would be forced to refer my case to county social services.

Along with my abysmal school record came drug experimentation—nothing hard, just what alcohol I could get my hands on and a stash of weed that Ken's son and I found. Final proof, I suppose, that I did know the difference between a tomato plant and marijuana.

For the first time in my life, I felt detached from Lindsay. She'd been married well over a year and had a toddler. There was something heroic about Lindsay's marriage—that after everything she'd witnessed, she'd ended up with someone who treated her well and had a decent job. Lindsay seemed genuinely happy. She was a good mom who doted on her young son. She had a little house not far from Mamaw's and seemed to be finding her way.

Though I felt happy for my sister, her new life heightened my sense of separation. For my entire existence, we had lived under the same roof, but now she lived in Middletown, and I lived with Ken about twenty miles away. While Lindsay built a life almost in opposition to the one she left behind—she would be a good mother, she would have a successful marriage (and only one)—I found myself mired in the things that both of us hated. While Lindsay and her new husband took trips to Florida and California, I was stuck in a stranger's house in Miamisburg, Ohio.

Chapter 9

Mamaw knew little of how this arrangement affected me, partly by design. During a long Christmas break, just a couple of months after I'd moved in with my new stepfather, I called her to complain. But when she answered, I could hear the voices of family in the background—my aunt, I thought, and cousin Gail, and perhaps some others. The background noise suggested holiday merriment, and I didn't have the heart to tell her what I had called to say: that I loathed living with these strangers and that everything that had made my life to that point tolerable—the reprieve of her house, the company of my sister—had apparently vanished. I asked her to tell everyone whose voice I heard in the background that I loved them, and then I hung up the phone and marched upstairs to watch TV. I had never felt so alone. Happily, I continued to attend Middletown's schools, which kept me in touch with my school friends and gave me an excuse to spend a few hours at Mamaw's. During active school sessions, I saw her a few times a week, and every time I did, she reminded me of the importance of doing well academically. She often remarked that if anyone in our family "made it," it would be me. I didn't have the heart to tell her what was really happening. I was supposed to be a lawyer or a doctor or a businessman, not a high school dropout. But I was much closer to dropping out than I was to anything else.

She learned the truth when Mom came to me one morning demanding a jar of clean urine. I had stayed at Mamaw's the night before and was getting ready for school when Mom walked in, frantic and out of breath. She had to submit to random urinalyses from the nursing board in order to keep her license, and someone had called that morning demanding a sample by the end of the day. Mamaw's piss was dirtied with a half dozen prescription drugs, so I was the only candidate.

Mom's demand came with a strong air of entitlement. She had no remorse, no sense that she was asking me to do something wrong. Nor was there any guilt over the fact that she had broken yet another promise to never use drugs.

I refused. Sensing my resistance, Mom transitioned. She became apologetic and desperate. She cried and begged. "I promise I'll do better. I promise." I had heard it many times before, and I didn't believe it even a little. Lindsay once told me that, above all, Mom was a survivor. She survived her childhood, she survived the men who came and went. She survived successive brushes with the law. And now she was doing everything she could to survive an encounter with the nursing board.

I exploded. I told Mom that if she wanted clean piss, she should stop fucking up her life and get it from her own bladder. I told Mamaw that enabling Mom made it worse and that if she had put her foot down thirty years earlier, then maybe Mom wouldn't be begging her son for clean piss. I told Mom that she was a shitty mother and I told Mamaw that she was a shitty mother, too. The color drained from Mamaw's face, and she refused to even look me in the eye. What I had said had clearly struck a nerve.

Though I meant these things, I also knew that my urine might not be clean. Mom collapsed onto the couch, crying quietly, but Mamaw wouldn't give in so easily, even though I'd wounded her with my criticism. I pulled Mamaw into the bathroom and whispered a confession—that I had smoked Ken's pot twice in the past few weeks. "I can't give it to her. If Mom takes my pee, we could both be in trouble."

First, Mamaw assuaged my fears. A couple of hits of pot over three weeks wouldn't show up on the screen, she told me. "Besides, you probably didn't know what the hell you were doing. You didn't inhale, even if you tried." Then she addressed the morality of it. "I know this isn't right, honey. But she's your mother and she's my daughter. And maybe, if we help her this time, she'll finally learn her lesson."

It was the eternal hope, the thing to which I couldn't say no. That hope drove me to voluntarily attend those many N.A. meetings, consume books on addiction, and participate in Mom's treatment to the fullest extent that I could. It had driven me to get in the car with her when I was twelve, knowing that her emotional state could lead her to do something she'd regret later. Mamaw never lost that hope, after more heartache and more disappointment than I could possibly fathom. Her life was a clinic in how to lose faith in people, but Mamaw always found a way to believe in the people she loved. So I don't regret relenting. Giving Mom that piss was wrong, but I'll never regret following Mamaw's lead. Her hope allowed her to forgive Papaw after the rough years of their marriage. And it convinced her to take me in when I needed her most.

Though I followed Mamaw's lead, something inside me broke that morning. I went to school red-eyed from crying and regretful that I'd helped. A few weeks earlier, I had sat with Mom at a Chinese buffet as she tried in vain to shovel food in her mouth. It's a memory that still makes my blood boil: Mom unable to open her eyes or close her mouth, spooning food in as it fell back on the plate. Other people stared at us, Ken was speechless, and Mom was oblivious. It was a prescription pain pill (or many of them) that had done this to her. I hated her for it and promised myself that if she ever did drugs again, I'd leave the house.

The urine episode was the last straw for Mamaw, too. When I came home from school, Mamaw told me that she wanted me to stay with her permanently, with no more moving in between. Mom seemed not to care: She needed a "break," she said, I supposed from being a mother. She and Ken didn't last much longer. By the end of sophomore year, she had moved out of his house and I had moved in with Mamaw, never to return to the homes of Mom and her men. At least she passed her piss test.

I didn't even have to pack, because much of what I owned remained at Mamaw's as I bounced from place to place. She didn't approve of me taking too many of my belongings to Ken's house, convinced that he and his kids might steal my socks and shirts. (Neither Ken nor his children ever stole from me.) Though I loved living with her, my new home tested my patience on many levels. I still harbored the insecurity that I was burdening her. More important, she was a hard woman to live with, quick-witted and sharp-tongued. If I didn't take out the garbage, she told me to "stop being a lazy piece of shit." When I forgot to do my homework, she called me "shit for brains" and reminded me that unless I studied, I'd amount to nothing. She demanded that

I play card games with her—usually gin rummy—and she never lost. "You are the worst fucking cardplayer I've ever met," she'd gloat. (That one didn't make me feel bad: She said it to everyone she beat, and she beat everyone at gin rummy.)

Years later, every single one of my relatives—Aunt Wee, Uncle Jimmy, even Lindsay—repeated some version of "Mamaw was really hard on you. Too hard." There were three rules in her house: Get good grades, get a job, and "get off your ass and help me." There was no set chore list; I just had to help her with whatever she was doing. And she never told me what to do—she just yelled at me if she did anything and I wasn't helping.

But we had a lot of fun. Mamaw had a much bigger bark than bite, at least with me. She once ordered me to watch a TV show with her on a Friday night, a creepy murder mystery, the type of show Mamaw loved to watch. At the climax of the show, during a moment designed to make the viewer jump, Mamaw flipped off the lights and screamed in my ear. She'd seen the episode before and knew what was coming. She made me sit there for forty-five minutes just so she could scare me at the appointed time.

The best part about living with Mamaw was that I began to understand what made her tick. Until then, I had resented how rarely we traveled to Kentucky after Mamaw Blanton's death. The decline in visits wasn't noticeable at first, but by the time I started middle school, we visited Kentucky only a few times a year for a few days at a time. Living with Mamaw, I learned that she and her sister, Rose—a woman of uncommon kindness—had a falling-out after their mother died. Mamaw had hoped that the old house would become a sort of family time share, while Rose had hoped that the house would go to her son and his family. Rose had a point: None of the siblings who lived in Ohio or

Indiana visited often enough, so it made sense to give the house to someone who would use it. But Mamaw feared that without a home base, her children and grandchildren would have no place to stay during their visits to Jackson. She, too, had a point.

I started to understand that Mamaw saw returning to Jackson as a duty to endure rather than a source of enjoyment. To me, Jackson was about my uncles, and chasing turtles, and finding peace from the instability that plagued my Ohio existence. Jackson gave me a shared home with Mamaw, a three-hour road trip to tell and listen to stories, and a place where everyone knew me as the grandson of the famous Jim and Bonnie Vance. Jackson was something much different to her. It was the place where she sometimes went hungry as a child, from which she ran in the wake of a teenage pregnancy scandal, and where so many of her friends had given their lives in the mines. I wanted to escape to Jackson; she had escaped from it.

In her old age, with limited mobility, Mamaw loved to watch TV. She preferred raunchy humor and epic dramas, so she had a lot of options. But her favorite show by far was the HBO mob story *The Sopranos*. Looking back, it's hardly surprising that a show about fiercely loyal, sometimes violent outsiders resonated with Mamaw. Change the names and dates, and the Italian Mafia starts to look a lot like the Hatfield-McCoy dispute back in Appalachia. The show's main character, Tony Soprano, was a violent killer, an objectively terrible person by almost any standard. But Mamaw respected his loyalty and the fact that he would go to any length to protect the honor of his family. Though he murdered countless enemies and drank excessively, the only criticism she ever levied against him involved his infidelity. "He's always sleeping around. I don't like that."

I also saw for the first time Mamaw's love of children, not as an object of her affection but as an observer of it. She often babysat for Lindsay's or Aunt Wee's young kids. One day she had both of Aunt Wee's girls for the day and Aunt Wee's dog in the back-yard. When the dog barked, Mamaw screamed, "Shut up, you son of a bitch." My cousin Bonnie Rose ran to the back door and began screaming over and over, "Son of a bitch! Son of a bitch!" Mamaw hobbled over to Bonnie Rose and scooped her up in her arms. "Shhh! You can't say that or you'll get me in trouble." But she was laughing so hard that she could barely get the words out. A few weeks later, I got home from school and asked Mamaw how her day had gone. She told me that she'd had a great day because she'd been watching Lindsay's son Kameron. "He asked me if he could say 'fuck' like I do. I told him yes, but only at my house." Then she chuckled quietly to herself. Regardless of how she felt, whether her emphysema made it difficult to breathe or her hip hurt so badly that she could barely walk, she never turned down an opportunity to "spend time with those babies," as she put it. Mamaw loved them, and I began to understand why she had always dreamed of becoming a lawyer for abused and neglected children.

At some point, Mamaw underwent major back surgery to help with the pain that made walking difficult. She landed in a nursing home for a few months to recover, forcing me to live alone, an experience that happily didn't last long. Every night she called Lindsay, Aunt Wee, or me and made the same re-quest: "I hate the damned food here. Can you go to Taco Bell and get me a bean burrito?" Indeed, Mamaw hated everything about the nursing home and once asked me to promise that if she ever faced a permanent stay, I'd take her .44 Magnum and put a bullet in her head. "Mamaw, you can't ask me to do that. I'd go to jail for the rest of my life." "Well," she said, pausing for a moment to reflect, "then get your hands on some arsenic. That way no one will know." Her back surgery, it turned out, was completely unnecessary. She had a broken hip, and as soon as a surgeon repaired it, she was back on her feet, though she used a walker or cane from then on. Now that I'm a lawyer, I marvel that we never considered a medical malpractice suit against the doctor who operated unnecessarily on her back. But Mamaw wouldn't have allowed it: She didn't believe in using the legal system until you had to.

Sometimes I'd see Mom every few days, and sometimes I'd go a couple of weeks without hearing from her at all. After one breakup, she spent a few months on Mamaw's couch, and we both enjoyed her company. Mom tried, in her own way: When she was working, she'd always give me money on paydays, almost certainly more than she could afford. For reasons I never quite understood, Mom equated money with affection. Perhaps she felt that I would never appreciate that she loved me unless she offered a wad of spending money. But I never cared about the money. I just wanted her to be healthy.

Not even my closest friends knew that I lived in my grandma's house. I recognized that though many of my peers lacked the traditional American family, mine was more nontraditional than most. And we were poor, a status Mamaw wore like a badge of honor but one I'd hardly come to grips with. I didn't wear clothes from Abercrombie & Fitch or American Eagle unless I'd received them for Christmas. When Mamaw picked me up from school, I'd ask her not to get out of the car lest my friends see her— wearing her uniform of baggy jeans and a men's T-shirt—with a giant menthol cigarette hanging from her lip. When people asked, I lied and told them that I lived with my mom, that she and I took care of my ailing grandmother. Even today, I still regret that far too many high school friends and acquaintances never knew Mamaw was the best thing that ever happened to me.

My junior year, I tested into the honors Advanced Math class—a hybrid of trigonometry, advanced algebra, and pre-calculus. The class's instructor, Ron Selby, enjoyed legendary status among the students for his brilliance and high demands. In twenty years, he had never missed a day of school. According to Middletown High School legend, a student called in a bomb threat during one of Selby's exams, hiding the explosive device in a bag in his locker. With the entire school evacuated outside, Selby marched into the school, retrieved the contents of the kid's locker, marched outside, and threw those contents into a trash can. "I've had that kid in class; he's not smart enough to make a functioning bomb," Selby told the police officers gathered at the school. "Now let my students go back to class to finish their exams."

Mamaw loved stories like this, and though she never met Selby, she admired him and encouraged me to follow his lead. Selby encouraged (but didn't require) his students to obtain advanced graphing calculators—the Texas Instruments model 89 was the latest and greatest. We didn't have cell phones, and we didn't have nice clothes, but Mamaw made sure that I had one of those graphing calculators. This taught me an important lesson about Mamaw's values, and it forced me to engage with school in a way I never had before. If Mamaw could drop $180 on a graphing calculator—she insisted that I spend none of my own money—then I had better take schoolwork more seriously. I owed it to her, and she reminded me of it constantly. "Have you finished your work for that Selby teacher?" "No, Mamaw, not yet." "You damn well better start. I didn't spend every penny I had on that little computer so you could fuck around all day."

Those three years with Mamaw—uninterrupted and alone—saved me. I didn't notice the causality of the change, how living with her turned my life around. I didn't notice that my grades began to improve immediately after I moved in. And I couldn't have known that I was making lifelong friends.

During that time, Mamaw and I started to talk about the problems in our community. Mamaw encouraged me to get a job—she told me that it would be good for me and that I needed to learn the value of a dollar. When her encouragement fell on deaf ears, she then demanded that I get a job, and so I did, as a cashier at Dillman's, a local grocery store.

Working as a cashier turned me into an amateur sociologist. A frenetic stress animated so many of our customers. One of our neighbors would walk in and yell at me for the smallest of transgressions—not smiling at her, or bagging the groceries too heavy one day or too light the next. Some came into the store in a hurry, pacing between aisles, looking frantically for a particular item. But others waded through the aisles deliberately, carefully marking each item off of their list. Some folks purchased a lot of canned and frozen food, while others consistently arrived at the checkout counter with carts piled high with fresh produce. The more harried a customer, the more they purchased precooked or frozen food, the more likely they were to be poor. And I knew they were poor because of the clothes they wore or because they purchased their food with food stamps. After a few months, I came home and asked Mamaw why only poor people bought baby formula. "Don't rich people have babies, too?" Mamaw had no answers, and it would be many years before I learned that rich folks are considerably more likely to breast-feed their children.

As my job taught me a little more about America's class divide, it also imbued me with a bit of resentment, directed toward both the wealthy and my own kind. The owners of Dillman's were old-fashioned, so they allowed people with good credit to run grocery tabs, some of which surpassed a thousand dollars. I knew that if any of my relatives walked in and ran up a bill of over a thousand dollars, they'd be asked to pay immediately. I hated the feeling that my boss counted my people as less trustworthy than those who took their groceries home in a Cadillac. But I got over it: One day, I told myself, I'll have my own damned tab.

I also learned how people gamed the welfare system. They'd buy two dozen-packs of soda with food stamps and then sell them at a discount for cash. They'd ring up their orders separately, buying food with food stamps, and beer, wine, and cigarettes with cash. They'd regularly go through the checkout line speaking on their cell phones. I could never understand why our lives felt like a struggle while those living off of government largesse enjoyed trinkets that I only dreamed about.

Mamaw listened intently to my experiences at Dillman's. We began to view much of our fellow working class with mistrust. Most of us were struggling to get by, but we made do, worked hard, and hoped for a better life. But a large minority was content to live off the dole. Every two weeks, I'd get a small paycheck and notice the line where federal and state income taxes were deducted from my wages. At least as often, our drug-addict neighbor would buy T-bone steaks, which I was too poor to buy for myself but was forced by Uncle Sam to buy for someone else.

This was my mind-set when I was seventeen, and though I'm far less angry today than I was then, it was my first indication that the policies of Mamaw's "party of the working man"—the Democrats—weren't all they were cracked up to be.

Political scientists have spent millions of words trying to explain how Appalachia and the South went from staunchly Democratic to staunchly Republican in less than a generation. Some blame race relations and the Democratic Party's embrace of the civil rights movement. Others cite religious faith and the hold that social conservatism has on evangelicals in that region. A big part of the explanation lies in the fact that many in the white working class saw precisely what I did, working at Dillman's. As far back as the 1970s, the white working class began to turn to Richard Nixon because of a perception that, as one man put it, government was "payin' people who are on welfare today doin' nothin'! They're laughin' at our society! And we're all hardworkin' people and we're gettin' laughed at for workin' every day!"[20]

At around that time, our neighbor—one of Mamaw and Papaw's oldest friends—registered the house next to ours for Section 8. Section 8 is a government program that offers low-income residents a voucher to rent housing. Mamaw's friend had little luck renting his property, but when he qualified his house for the Section 8 voucher, he virtually assured that would change. Mamaw saw it as a betrayal, ensuring that "bad" people would move into the neighborhood and drive down property values.

Despite our efforts to draw bright lines between the working and nonworking poor, Mamaw and I recognized that we shared a lot in common with those whom we thought gave our people a bad name. Those Section 8 recipients looked a lot like us. The matriarch of the first family to move in next door was born in

Kentucky but moved north at a young age as her parents sought a better life. She'd gotten involved with a couple of men, each of whom had left her with a child but no support. She was nice, and so were her kids. But the drugs and the late-night fighting revealed troubles that too many hillbilly transplants knew too well. Confronted with such a realization of her own family's struggle, Mamaw grew frustrated and angry.

From that anger sprang Bonnie Vance the social policy expert: "She's a lazy whore, but she wouldn't be if she was forced to get a job"; "I hate those fuckers for giving these people the money to move into our neighborhood." She'd rant against the people we'd see in the grocery store: "I can't understand why people who've worked all their lives scrape by while these deadbeats buy liquor and cell phone coverage with our tax money."

These were bizarre views for my bleeding-heart grandma. And if she blasted the government for doing too much one day, she'd blast it for doing too little the next. The government, after all, was just helping poor people find a place to live, and my grandma loved the idea of anyone helping the poor. She had no philosophical objection to Section 8 vouchers. So the Democrat in her would resurface. She'd rant about the lack of jobs and wonder aloud whether that was why our neighbor couldn't find a good man. In her more compassionate moments, Mamaw asked if it made any sense that our society could afford aircraft carriers but not drug treatment facilities—like Mom's—for everyone. Sometimes she'd criticize the faceless rich, whom she saw as far too unwilling to carry their fair share of the social burden. Mamaw saw every ballot failure of the local school improvement tax (and there were many) as an indictment of our society's failure to provide a quality education to kids like me.

Mamaw's sentiments occupied wildly different parts of the political spectrum. Depending on her mood, Mamaw was a radical conservative or a European-style social Democrat. Because of this, I initially assumed that Mamaw was an unreformed simpleton and that as soon as she opened her mouth about policy or politics, I might as well close my ears. Yet I quickly realized that in Mamaw's contradictions lay great wisdom. I had spent so long just surviving my world, but now that I had a little space to observe it, I began to see the world as Mamaw did. I was scared, confused, angry, and heartbroken. I'd blame large businesses for closing up shop and moving overseas, and then I'd wonder if I might have done the same thing. I'd curse our government for not helping enough, and then I'd wonder if, in its attempts to help, it actually made the problem worse.

Mamaw could spew venom like a Marine Corps drill instructor, but what she saw in our community didn't just piss her off. It broke her heart. Behind the drugs, and the fighting matches, and the financial struggles, these were people with serious problems, and they were hurting. Our neighbors had a kind of desperate sadness in their lives. You'd see it in how the mother would grin but never really smile, or in the jokes that the teenage girl told about her mother "smacking the shit out of her." I knew what awkward humor like this was meant to conceal because I'd used it in the past. Grin and bear it, says the adage. If anyone appreciated this, Mamaw did.

The problems of our community hit close to home. Mom's struggles weren't some isolated incident. They were replicated, replayed, and relived by many of the people who, like us, had moved hundreds of miles in search of a better life. There was no end in sight. Mamaw had thought she escaped the poverty of the hills, but the poverty—emotional, if not financial—had followed her. Something had made her later years eerily similar to her earliest ones. What was happening? What were our neighbor's teenage daughter's prospects? Certainly the odds were against her, with a home life like that. This raised the question: What would happen to me?

I was unable to answer these questions in a way that didn't implicate something deep within the place I called home. What I knew is that other people didn't live like we did. When I visited Uncle Jimmy, I did not wake to the screams of neighbors. In Aunt Wee and Dan's neighborhood, homes were beautiful and lawns well manicured, and police came around to smile and wave but never to load someone's mom or dad in the back of their cruiser.

So I wondered what was different about us—not just me and my family but our neighborhood and our town and everyone from Jackson to Middletown and beyond. When Mom was arrested a couple of years earlier, the neighborhood's porches and front yards filled with spectators; there's no embarrassment like waving to the neighbors right after the cops have carted your mother off. Mom's exploits were undoubtedly extreme, but all of us had seen the show before with different neighbors. These sorts of things had their own rhythm. A mild screaming match might invite a few cracked shutters or peeking eyes behind the shades. If things escalated a bit, bedrooms would illuminate as people awoke to investigate the commotion. And if things got out of hand, the police would come and take someone's drunk dad or unhinged mom down to the city building. That building housed the tax collector, the public utilities, and even a small museum, but all the kids in my neighborhood knew it as the home of Middletown's short-term jail.

I consumed books about social policy and the working poor. One book in particular, a study by eminent sociologist William Julius Wilson called *The Truly Disadvantaged*, struck a nerve. I was sixteen the first time I read it, and though I didn't fully understand it all, I grasped the core thesis. As millions migrated north to factory jobs, the communities that sprouted up around those factories were vibrant but fragile: When the factories shut their doors, the people left behind were trapped in towns and cities that could no longer support such large populations with high-quality work. Those who could—generally the well educated, wealthy, or well connected—left, leaving behind communities of poor people. These remaining folks were the "truly disadvantaged"—unable to find good jobs on their own and surrounded by communities that offered little in the way of connections or social support.

Wilson's book spoke to me. I wanted to write him a letter and tell him that he had described my home perfectly. That it resonated so personally is odd, however, because he wasn't writing about the hillbilly transplants from Appalachia—he was writing about black people in the inner cities. The same was true of Charles Murray's seminal *Losing Ground*, another book about black folks that could have been written about hillbillies— which addressed the way our government encouraged social decay through the welfare state.

Though insightful, neither of these books fully answered the questions that plagued me: Why didn't our neighbor leave that abusive man? Why did she spend her money on drugs? Why couldn't she see that her behavior was destroying her daughter? Why were all of these things happening not just to our neighbor but to my mom? It would be years before I learned that no single book, or expert, or field could fully explain the problems of hillbillies in modern America. Our elegy is a sociological one, yes, but it is also about psychology and community and culture and faith.

During my junior year of high school, our neighbor Pattie called her landlord to report a leaky roof. The landlord arrived and found Pattie topless, stoned, and unconscious on her living room couch. Upstairs the bathtub was overflowing—hence, the leaking roof. Pattie had apparently drawn herself a bath, taken a few prescription painkillers, and passed out. The top floor of her home and many of her family's possessions were ruined. This is the reality of our community. It's about a naked druggie destroying what little of value exists in her life. It's about children who lose their toys and clothes to a mother's addiction.

Another neighbor lived alone in a big pink house. She was a recluse, a neighborhood mystery. She came outside only to smoke. She never said hello, and her lights were always off. She and her husband had divorced, and her children had landed in jail. She was extremely obese—as a child, I used to wonder if she hated the outdoors because she was too heavy to move.

There were the neighbors down the street, a younger woman with a toddler and her middle-aged boyfriend. The boyfriend worked, and the woman spent her days watching *The Young and the Restless*. Her young son was adorable, and he loved Mamaw. At all times of the day—one time, past midnight—he would wander to her doorstep and ask for a snack. His mother had all the time in the world, but she couldn't keep a close enough watch on her child to prevent him from straying into the homes of strangers. Sometimes his diaper would need changing. Mamaw once called social services on the woman, hoping they'd somehow rescue the young boy. They did nothing. So Mamaw used my nephew's diapers and kept a watchful eye on the neighborhood, always looking for signs of her "little buddy."

My sister's friend lived in a small duplex with her mother (a welfare queen if one ever existed). She had seven siblings, most of them from the same father—which was, unfortunately, a rarity. Her mother had never held a job and seemed interested "only in breeding," as Mamaw put it. Her kids never had a chance. One ended up in an abusive relationship that produced a child before the mom was old enough to purchase cigarettes. The oldest overdosed on drugs and was arrested not long after he graduated from high school.

This was my world: a world of truly irrational behavior. We spend our way into the poorhouse. We buy giant TVs and iPads. Our children wear nice clothes thanks to high-interest credit cards and payday loans. We purchase homes we don't need, refinance them for more spending money, and declare bankruptcy, often leaving them full of garbage in our wake. Thrift is inimical to our being. We spend to pretend that we're upper-class. And when the dust clears—when bankruptcy hits or a family member bails us out of our stupidity—there's nothing left over. Nothing for the kids' college tuition, no investment to grow our wealth, no rainy-day fund if someone loses her job. We know we shouldn't spend like this. Sometimes we beat ourselves up over it, but we do it anyway.

Our homes are a chaotic mess. We scream and yell at each other like we're spectators at a football game. At least one member of the family uses drugs—sometimes the father, sometimes the mother, sometimes both. At especially stressful times, we'll hit and punch each other, all in front of the rest of the family, including young children; much of the time, the neighbors hear what's happening. A bad day is when the neighbors call the police to stop the drama. Our kids go to foster care but never stay for long. We apologize to our kids. The kids believe we're really sorry, and we are. But then we act just as mean a few days later.

We don't study as children, and we don't make our kids study when we're parents. Our kids perform poorly in school. We might get angry with them, but we never give them the tools— like peace and quiet at home—to succeed. Even the best and brightest will likely go to college close to home, if they survive the war zone in their own home. "I don't care if you got into Notre Dame," we say. "You can get a fine, cheap education at the community college." The irony is that for poor people like us, an education at Notre Dame is both cheaper and finer.

We choose not to work when we should be looking for jobs. Sometimes we'll get a job, but it won't last. We'll get fired for tardiness, or for stealing merchandise and selling it on eBay, or for having a customer complain about the smell of alcohol on our breath, or for taking five thirty-minute restroom breaks per shift. We talk about the value of hard work but tell ourselves that the reason we're not working is some perceived unfairness: Obama shut down the coal mines, or all the jobs went to the Chinese. These are the lies we tell ourselves to solve the cognitive dissonance—the broken connection between the world we see and the values we preach.

We talk to our children about responsibility, but we never walk the walk. It's like this: For years I'd dreamed of owning a German shepherd puppy. Somehow Mom found me one. But he was our fourth dog, and I had no clue how to train him. Within a

few years, all of them had vanished—given to the police department or to a family friend. After saying goodbye to the fourth
dog, our hearts harden. We learn not to grow too attached.

Our eating and exercise habits seem designed to send us to
an early grave, and it's working: In certain parts of Kentucky,
local life expectancy is sixty-seven, a full decade and a half below
what it is in nearby Virginia. A recent study found that unique
among all ethnic groups in the United States, the life expectancy
of working-class white folks is going down. We eat Pillsbury cin-
namon rolls for breakfast, Taco Bell for lunch, and McDonald's
for dinner. We rarely cook, even though it's cheaper and better
for the body and soul. Exercise is confined to the games we play
as children. We see people jog on the streets only if we leave our
homes for the military or for college in some distant place.

Not all of the white working class struggles. I knew even
as a child that there were two separate sets of mores and social
pressures. My grandparents embodied one type: old-fashioned,
quietly faithful, self-reliant, hardworking. My mother and, increasingly, the entire neighborhood embodied another: consum-
erist, isolated, angry, distrustful.

There were (and remain) many who lived by my grandparents'
code. Sometimes you saw it in the subtlest of ways: the old neighbor who diligently tended her garden even as her neighbors let
their homes rot from the inside out; the young woman who grew
up with my mom, who returned to the neighborhood every day
to help her mother navigate old age. I say this not to romanticize
my grandparents' way of life—which, as I've observed, was rife
with problems—but to note that many in our community may
have struggled but did so successfully. There are many intact
families, many dinners shared in peaceful homes, many children

studying hard and believing they'll claim their own American Dream. Many of my friends have built successful lives and happy families in Middletown or nearby. They are not the problem, and if you believe the statistics, the children of these intact homes have plenty of reason for optimism.

I always straddled those two worlds. Thanks to Mamaw, I never saw only the worst of what our community offered, and I believe that saved me. There was always a safe place and a loving embrace if ever I needed it. Our neighbors' kids couldn't say the same.

One Sunday, Mamaw agreed to watch Aunt Wee's kids for several hours. Aunt Wee dropped them off at ten. I had to work the dreaded eleven A.M. to eight P.M. shift at the grocery store. I hung out with the kids for about forty-five minutes, then left at ten-forty-five for work. I was unusually upset—devastated, even—to leave them. I wanted nothing more than to spend the day with Mamaw and the babies. I told Mamaw that, and instead of telling me to "quit your damn whining" like I expected, she told me she wished that I could stay home, too. It was a rare moment of empathy. "But if you want the sort of work where you can spend the weekends with your family, you've got to go to college and make something of yourself." That was the essence of Mamaw's genius. She didn't just preach and cuss and demand. She showed me what was possible—a peaceful Sunday afternoon with the people I loved—and made sure I knew how to get there.

Reams of social science attest to the positive effect of a loving and stable home. I could cite a dozen studies suggesting that Mamaw's home offered me not just a short-term haven but also hope for a better life. Entire volumes are devoted to the phenomenon of "resilient children"—kids who prosper despite an unstable home because they have the social support of a loving adult.

I know Mamaw was good for me not because some Harvard psychologist says so but because I felt it. Consider my life before I moved in with Mamaw. In the middle of third grade, we left Middletown and my grandparents to live in Preble County with Bob; at the end of fourth grade, we left Preble County to live in a Middletown duplex on the 200 block of McKinley Street; at the end of fifth grade, we left the 200 block of McKinley Street to move to the 300 block of McKinley Street, and by that time Chip was a regular in our home, though he never lived with us; at the end of sixth grade, we remained on the 300 block of McKinley Street, but Chip had been replaced by Steve (and there were many discussions about moving in with Steve); at the end of seventh grade, Matt had taken Steve's place, Mom was preparing to move in with Matt, and Mom hoped that I would join her in Dayton; at the end of eighth grade, she demanded that I move to Dayton, and after a brief detour at my dad's house, I acquiesced; at the end of ninth grade, I moved in with Ken—a complete stranger—and his three kids. On top of all that were the drugs, the domestic violence case, children's services prying into our lives, and Papaw dying.

Today, even remembering that period long enough to write it down invokes an intense, indescribable anxiety in me. Not long ago, I noticed that a Facebook friend (an acquaintance from high school with similarly deep hillbilly roots) was constantly changing boyfriends—going in and out of relationships, posting pictures of one guy one week and another three weeks later, fighting on social media with her new fling until the relationship publicly imploded. She is my age with four children, and when she posted that she had finally found a man who would treat her well (a refrain I'd seen many times before), her thirteen-year-old daughter commented: "Just stop. I just want you and this to stop." I wish I could hug that little girl, because I know how she feels. For seven long years, I just wanted it to stop. I didn't care so much about the fighting, the screaming, or even the drugs. I just wanted a home, and I wanted to stay there, and I wanted these goddamned strangers to stay the fuck out.

Now consider the sum of my life after I moved in with Mamaw permanently. At the end of tenth grade, I lived with Mamaw, in her house, with no one else. At the end of eleventh grade, I lived with Mamaw, in her house, with no one else. At the end of twelfth grade, I lived with Mamaw, in her house, with no one else. I could say that the peace of Mamaw's home gave me a safe space to do my homework. I could say that the absence of fighting and instability let me focus on school and my job. I could say that spending all of my time in the same house with the same person made it easier for me to form lasting friendships with people at school. I could say that having a job and learning a bit about the world helped clarify precisely what I wanted out of my own life. In hindsight, those explanations make sense, and I am certain that a bit of truth lies in each.

I'm sure that a sociologist and a psychologist, sitting in a room together, could explain why I lost interest in drugs, why my grades improved, why I aced the SAT, and why I found a couple of teachers who inspired me to love learning. But what I remember most of all is that I was *happy*—I no longer feared the school bell at the end of the day, I knew where I'd be living the next month, and no one's romantic decisions affected my life. And out of that happiness came so many of the opportunities I've had for the past twelve years.

Chapter 10

During my last year of high school, I tried out for the varsity golf team. For about a year, I'd taken golf lessons from an old golf pro. The summer before senior year, I got a job at a local golf course so I could practice for free. Mamaw never showed any interest in sports, but she encouraged me to learn golf because "that's where rich people do business." Though wise in her own way, Mamaw knew little about the business habits of rich people, and I told her as much. "Shut up, you fucker," she told me. "Everybody knows rich people love to golf." But when I practiced my swing in the house (I didn't use a ball, so the only damage I did was to the floor) she demanded that I stop ruining her carpet. "But, Mamaw," I protested sarcastically, "if you don't let me practice, I'll never get to do any business on the golf course. I might as well drop out of high school now and get a job bagging groceries." "You smart-ass. If I wasn't crippled, I'd get up right now and smack your head and ass together."

So she helped me pay for my lessons and asked her baby brother (my uncle Gary), the youngest of the Blanton boys, to find me some old clubs. He delivered a nice set of MacGregors, better than anything we could have afforded on our own, and I practiced as often as I could. By the time golf tryouts rolled around, I had mastered enough of a golf swing not to embarrass myself.

I didn't make the team, though I did show enough improvement to justify practicing with my friends who had made the team, and that was all I really wanted. I learned that Mamaw was right: Golf was a rich person's game. At the course where I worked, few of our customers came from Middletown's working-class neighborhoods. On my first day of golf practice, I showed up in dress shoes, thinking that was what golf shoes were. When an enterprising young bully noticed before the first tee that I was wearing a pair of Kmart brown loafers, he proceeded to mock me mercilessly for the next four hours. I resisted the urge to bury my putter in his goddamned ear, remembering Mamaw's sage advice to "act like you've been there." (A note about hillbilly loyalty: Reminded of that story recently, Lindsay launched into a tirade about how much of a loser the kid was. The incident occurred thirteen years ago.)

I knew in the back of my mind that decisions were coming about my future. All of my friends planned to go to college; that I had such motivated friends was due to Mamaw's influence. By the time I was in seventh grade, many of my neighborhood friends were already smoking weed. Mamaw found out and forbade me to see any of them. I recognize that most kids ignore instructions like these, but most kids don't receive them from the likes of Bonnie Vance. She promised that if she saw me in the presence of any person on the banned list, she would run him over with her car. "No one would ever find out," she whispered menacingly.

With my friends headed for college, I figured I'd do the same. I scored well enough on the SAT to overcome my earlier bad grades, and I knew that the only two schools I had any interest in attending—Ohio State and Miami University—would both accept me. A few months before I graduated, I had (admittedly, with little thought) settled on Ohio State. A large package arrived in the mail, filled with financial aid information from the university. There was talk of Pell Grants, subsidized loans, unsubsidized loans, scholarships, and something called "work-study." It was all so exciting, if only Mamaw and I could figure out what it meant. We puzzled over the forms for hours before concluding that I could purchase a decent home in Middletown with the debt I'd incur to go to college. We hadn't actually started the forms yet—that would require another herculean effort on another day.

Excitement turned to apprehension, but I reminded myself that college was an investment in my future. "It's the only damned thing worth spending money on right now," Mamaw said. She was right, but as I worried less about the financial aid forms, I began to worry for another reason: I wasn't ready. Not all investments are good investments. All of that debt, and for what? To get drunk all the time and earn terrible grades? Doing well in college required grit, and I had far too little of it.

My high school record left much to be desired: dozens of absences and tardy arrivals, and no school activities to speak of. I was undoubtedly on an upward trajectory, but even toward the end of high school, C's in easy classes revealed a kid unprepared for the rigors of advanced education. In Mamaw's house, I was healing, yet as we combed through those financial aid papers, I couldn't shake the feeling that I had a long way to go.

Everything about the unstructured college experience terrified me—from feeding myself healthy food to paying my own bills. I'd never done any of those things. But I knew that I wanted more out of my life. I knew that I wanted to excel in college, get a good job, and give my family the things I'd never had. I just wasn't ready to start that journey. That's when my cousin Rachael—a Marine Corps veteran—advised that I consider the Corps: "They'll whip your ass into shape." Rachael was Uncle Jimmy's oldest daughter, and thus the dean of our generation of grandchildren. All of us, even Lindsay, looked up to Rachael, so her advice carried enormous weight.

The 9/11 attacks had occurred only a year earlier, during my junior year of high school; like any self-respecting hillbilly, I considered heading to the Middle East to kill terrorists. But the prospect of military service—the screaming drill instructors, the constant exercise, the separation from my family—frightened me. Until Rachael told me to talk to a recruiter—implicitly arguing that she thought I could handle it—joining the Marines seemed as plausible as flying to Mars. Now, just weeks before I owed a tuition deposit to Ohio State, I could think of nothing but the Marine Corps.

So one Saturday in late March, I walked into a military recruiter's office and asked him about the Marine Corps. He didn't try to sell me on anything. He told me I'd make very little money and I might even go to war. "But they'll teach you about leadership, and they'll turn you into a disciplined young man." This piqued my interest, but the notion of J.D. the U.S. Marine still inspired disbelief. I was a pudgy, longhaired kid. When our gym teacher told us to run a mile, I'd walk at least half. I had never woken up before six A.M. And here was this organization promising that I'd rise regularly at five A.M. and run multiple miles per day.

I went home and considered my options. I reminded myself that my country needed me, and that I'd always regret not participating in America's newest war. I thought about the GI Bill and how it would help me trade indebtedness for financial freedom. I knew that, most of all, I had no other choice. There was college, or nothing, or the Marines, and I didn't like either of the first two options. Four years in the Marines, I told myself, would help me become the person I wanted to be. But I didn't want to leave home. Lindsay had just had her second kid, an adorable little girl, and was expecting a third, and my nephew was still a toddler. Lori's kids were still babies, too. The more I thought about it, the less I wanted to do it. And I knew that if I waited too long, I'd talk myself out of enlisting. So two weeks later, as the Iraq crisis turned into the Iraq war, I signed my name on a dotted line and promised the Marine Corps the first four years of my adult life.

At first my family scoffed. The Marines weren't for me, and people let me know it. Eventually, knowing I wouldn't change my mind, everyone came around, and a few even seemed excited. Everyone, that is, save Mamaw. She tried every manner of persuasion: "You're a fucking idiot; they'll chew you up and spit you out." "Who's going to take care of me?" "You're too stupid for the Marines." "You're too smart for the Marines." "With everything that's going on in the world, you'll get your head blown off." "Don't you want to be around for Lindsay's kids?" "I'm worried, and I don't want you to go." Though she came to accept the decision, she never liked it. Shortly before I left for boot camp, the recruiter visited to speak with my fragile grandmother. She met him outside, stood up as straight as she could, and glowered at him. "Set one foot on my fucking porch, and I'll blow it off," she advised. "I thought she might be serious," he later told me. So they had their talk while he stood in the front yard.

My greatest fear when I left for boot camp wasn't that I'd be killed in Iraq or that I'd fail to make the cut. I hardly worried about those things. But when Mom, Lindsay, and Aunt Wee drove me to the bus that would take me to the airport and on to boot camp from there, I imagined my life four years later. And I saw a world without my grandmother in it. Something inside me *knew* that she wouldn't survive my time in the Marines. I'd never come home again, at least not permanently. Home was Middletown with Mamaw in it. And by the time I finished with the Marines, Mamaw would be gone.

Marine Corps boot camp lasts thirteen weeks, each with a new training focus. The night I arrived in Parris Island, South Carolina, an angry drill instructor greeted my group as we disembarked from the plane. He ordered us onto a bus; after a short trip, another drill instructor ordered us off the bus and onto the famed "yellow footprints." Over the next six hours, I was poked and prodded by medical personnel, assigned equipment and uniforms, and lost all of my hair. We were allowed one phone call, so I naturally called Mamaw and read off of the card they gave me: "I have arrived safely at Parris Island. I will send my address soon. Goodbye." "Wait, you little shithead. Are you okay?" "Sorry, Mamaw, can't talk. But yes, I'm okay. I'll write as soon as I can." The drill instructor, overhearing my two extra lines of conversation, asked sarcastically whether I'd made enough time "for her to tell you a fucking story." That was the first day.

There are no phone calls in boot camp. I was allowed only

one, to call Lindsay when her half brother died. I realized, through letters, how much my family loved me. While most other recruits—that's what they called us; we had to earn the title "marine" by completing the rigors of boot camp—received a letter every day or two, I sometimes received a half dozen each night. Mamaw wrote every day, sometimes several times, offering extended thoughts on what was wrong with the world in some and few-sentence streams of consciousness in others. Most of all, Mamaw wanted to know how my days were going and reassure me. Recruiters told families that what most of us needed were words of encouragement, and Mamaw delivered that in spades. As I struggled with screaming drill instructors and physical fitness routines that pushed my out-of-shape body to its limits, I read every day that Mamaw was proud of me, that she loved me, and that she knew I wouldn't give up. Thanks to either my wisdom or inherited hoarder tendencies, I managed to keep nearly every one of the letters I received from my family.

Many of them shed an interesting light on the home I left behind. A letter from Mom, asking me what I might need and telling me how proud she is of me. "I was babysitting [Lindsay's kids]," she reports. "They played with slugs outside. They squeezed one and killed it. But I threw it away and told them they didn't because Kam got a little upset, thinking he killed it." This is Mom at her best: loving and funny, a woman who delighted in her grandchildren. In the same letter, a reference to Greg, likely a boyfriend who has since disappeared from my memory. And an insight into our sense of normalcy: "Mandy's husband Terry," she starts, referencing a friend of hers, "was arrested on a probation violation and sent to prison. So they are all doing OK."

Lindsay also wrote often, sending multiple letters in the same envelope, each on a different-colored piece of paper, with instructions on the back—"Read this one second; this is the last one." Every single letter contained some reference to her kids. I learned of my oldest niece's successful potty training; my nephew's soccer matches; my younger niece's early smiles and first efforts to reach for things. After a lifetime of shared triumphs and tragedies, we both adored her kids more than anything else. Almost all of the letters I sent home asked her to "kiss the babies and tell them that I love them."

Cut off for the first time from home and family, I learned a lot about myself and my culture. Contrary to conventional wisdom, the military is not a landing spot for low-income kids with no other options. The sixty-nine members of my boot camp platoon included black, white, and Hispanic kids; rich kids from upstate New York and poor kids from West Virginia; Catholics, Jews, Protestants, and even a few atheists.

I was naturally drawn to those like me. "The person I talk to most," I wrote to my family in my first letter home, "is from Leslie County, Kentucky. He talks like he's from Jackson. I was telling him how much bullshit it was that Catholics got all the free time they did. They get it because of the way the church schedule works. He is definitely a country kid, 'cause he said, 'What's a Catholic?' And I told him that it was just another form of Christianity, and he said, 'I might have to try that out.'" Mamaw understood precisely where he came from. "Down in that part of Kentucky, everybody's a snake handler," she wrote back, only partially joking.

During my time away, Mamaw showed vulnerability that I'd never seen before. Whenever she received a letter from me, she would call my aunt or sister, demanding that someone come to her house immediately and interpret my chicken scratch. "I love you a big bunch and I miss you a bunch I forget you aren't here I think you will come down the stairs and I can holler at you it is just a feeling you aren't really gone. My hands hurt today that arthritis I guess. . . . I'll go for now write more later love you please take care." Mamaw's letters never contained the necessary punctuation and always included some articles, usually from *Reader's Digest*, to occupy my time.

She could still be classic Mamaw: mean and ferociously loyal. About a month into my training, I had a nasty exchange with a drill instructor, who took me aside for a half hour, forcing me to alternate jumping jacks, sit-ups, and short sprints until I was completely exhausted. It was par for the course in boot camp, something nearly everyone faced at one point or another. If anything, I was lucky to have avoided it for so long. "Dearest J.D.," Mamaw wrote when she learned of the incident, "I must say I have been waiting for them dick face bastards to start on you— and now they have. Words aren't invented to describe how they piss me off. . . . You just keep on doing the best you can do and keep thinking about this stupid asshole with an IQ of 2 thinking he is Bobby bad ass but he wears girls underwear. I hate all of them." When I read that outburst, I figured Mamaw had gotten it all off her chest. But the next day, she had more to say: "Hello sweet heart all I can think about is them dicks screaming at you that is my job not them fuckers. Just kidding I know you will be what ever you want to be because you are smart something they aren't and they know it I hate them all really hate their guts. Screaming is part of the game they play . . . you carry on as best you can you will come out ahead." I had the meanest old hillbilly staunchly in my corner, even if she was hundreds of miles away.

In boot camp, mealtime is a marvel of efficiency. You walk through a cafeteria line, holding your tray for the service staff. They drop *all* of the day's offerings on your plate, both because you're afraid to speak up about your least favorite items and because you're so hungry that you'd gladly eat a dead horse. You sit down, and without looking at your plate (that would be unprofessional) or moving your head (that would also be unprofessional), you shovel food into your mouth until you're told to stop. The entire process takes no longer than eight minutes, and if you're not quite full by the end, you certainly suffer from indigestion (which feels about the same).

The only discretionary part of the exercise is dessert, set aside on small plates at the end of the assembly line. During the first meal of boot camp, I grabbed the offered piece of cake and marched to my seat. *If nothing else tastes good,* I thought, *this cake shall certainly be the exception.* Then my drill instructor, a skinny white man with a Tennessee twang, stepped in front of me. He looked me up and down with his small, intense eyes and offered a query: "You really need that cake, don't you, fat-ass?" I prepared to answer, but the question was apparently rhetorical, as he smacked the cake out of my hands and moved on to his next victim. I never grabbed the cake again.

There was an important lesson here, but not one about food or self-control or nutrition. If you'd told me that I'd react to such an insult by cleaning up the cake and heading back to my seat, I'd never have believed you. The trials of my youth instilled a debilitating self-doubt. Instead of congratulating myself on having overcome some obstacles, I worried that I'd *be* overcome by the next ones. Marine Corps boot camp, with its barrage of challenges big and small, began to teach me I had underestimated myself.

Marine Corps boot camp is set up as a life-defining challenge. From the day you arrive, no one calls you by your first name. You're not allowed to say "I" because you're taught to mistrust your own individuality. Every question begins with "This recruit"—This recruit needs to use the head (the bathroom); This recruit needs to visit the corpsman (the doctor). The few idiots who arrive at boot camp with Marine Corps tattoos are mercilessly berated. At every turn, recruits are reminded that they are worthless until they finish boot camp and earn the title "marine." Our platoon started with eighty-three, and by the time we finished, sixty-nine remained. Those who dropped out—mostly for medical reasons—served to reinforce the worthiness of the challenge.

Every time the drill instructor screamed at me and I stood proudly; every time I thought I'd fall behind during a run and kept up; every time I learned to do something I thought impossible, like climb the rope, I came a little closer to believing in myself. Psychologists call it "learned helplessness" when a person believes, as I did during my youth, that the choices I made had no effect on the outcomes in my life. From Middletown's world of small expectations to the constant chaos of our home, life had taught me that I had no control. Mamaw and Papaw had saved me from succumbing entirely to that notion, and the Marine Corps broke new ground. If I had learned helplessness at home, the Marines were teaching learned willfulness.

The day I graduated from boot camp was the proudest of my life. An entire crew of hillbillies showed up for my graduation—eighteen in total—including Mamaw, sitting in a wheelchair, buried underneath a few blankets, looking frailer than I remembered. I showed everyone around base, feeling like I had just won the lottery, and when I was released for a ten-day leave the next day, we caravanned back to Middletown.

On my first day home from boot camp, I walked into the barbershop of my grandfather's old friend. Marines have to keep their hair short, and I didn't want to slack just because no one was watching. For the first time, the corner barber—a dying breed even though I didn't know it at the time—greeted me as an adult. I sat in his chair, told some dirty jokes (most of which I'd learned only weeks earlier), and shared some boot camp stories. When he was about my age, he was drafted into the army to fight in Korea, so we traded some barbs about the Army and the Marines. After the haircut, he refused to take my money and told me to stay safe. He'd cut my hair before, and I'd walked by his shop nearly every day for eighteen years. Yet it was the first time he'd ever shaken my hand and treated me as an equal.

I had a lot of those experiences shortly after boot camp. In those first days as a marine—all spent in Middletown—every interaction was a revelation. I'd shed forty-five pounds, so many of the people I knew barely recognized me. My friend Nate—who would later serve as one of my groomsmen—did a double take when I extended my hand at a local mall. Perhaps I carried myself a little differently. My old hometown seemed to think so.

The new perspective went both ways. Many of the foods that I ate once now violated the fitness standards of a marine. In Mamaw's house, everything was fried—chicken, pickles, tomatoes. That bologna sandwich on toast with crumbled potato chips as topping no longer appeared healthy. Blackberry cobbler, once considered as healthy as any dish built around fruit (blackberries) and grains (flour), lost its luster. I began asking questions I'd never asked before: Is there added sugar? Does this meat have a lot of saturated fat? How much salt? It was just food, but I was already realizing that I'd never look at Middletown the same way again. In a few short months, the Marine Corps had already changed my perspective.

I soon left home for a permanent assignment in the Marine Corps, and life at home continued on apace. I tried to return as often as I could, and with long weekends and generous Marine Corps leave, I usually saw my family every few months. The kids looked a bit bigger every time I saw them, and Mom moved in with Mamaw not long after I left for boot camp, though she didn't plan to stay. Mamaw's health seemed to improve: She was walking better and even putting on a bit of weight. Lindsay and Aunt Wee, as well as their families, were healthy and happy. My greatest fear before I left was that some tragedy would befall my family while I was away, and I'd be unable to help. Luckily, that wasn't happening.

In January 2005, I learned that my unit would head to Iraq a few months later. I was both excited and nervous. Mamaw fell silent when I called to tell her. After a few uncomfortable seconds of dead air, she said only that she hoped the war would end before I had to leave. Though we spoke on the phone every few days, we never spoke of Iraq, even as winter turned to spring and everyone knew I'd be leaving for war that summer. I could tell that Mamaw didn't want to talk or think about it, and I obliged.

Mamaw was old, frail, and sick. I no longer lived with her, and I was preparing to go fight a war. Though her health had improved somewhat since I'd left for the Marines, she still took a dozen medications and made quarterly trips to the hospital for various ailments. When AK Steel—which provided health care for Mamaw as Papaw's widow—announced that they were increasing her premiums, Mamaw simply couldn't afford them. She barely survived as it was, and she needed three hundred dollars extra per month. She told me as much one day, and I immediately volunteered to cover the costs. She had never accepted anything from me—not money from my paycheck at Dillman's; not a share of my boot camp earnings. But she accepted my three hundred a month, and that's how I knew she was desperate.

I didn't make a lot of money myself—probably a thousand dollars a month after taxes, though the Marines gave me a place to stay and food to eat, so that money went far. I also made extra money playing online poker. Poker was in my blood—I'd played with pennies and dimes with Papaw and my great-uncles as far back as I could remember—and the online poker craze at the time made it basically free money. I played ten hours a week on small-stakes tables, earning four hundred dollars a month. I had planned to save that money, but instead I gave it to Mamaw for her health insurance. Mamaw, naturally, worried that I had picked up a gambling habit and was playing cards in some mountain trailer with a bunch of card-sharking hillbillies, but I assured her that it was online and legitimate. "Well, you know I don't understand the fucking Internet. Just don't turn to booze and women. That's always what happens to dipshits who get caught up in gambling."

Mamaw and I both loved the movie *Terminator 2*. We probably watched it together five or six times. Mamaw saw Arnold Schwarzenegger as the embodiment of the American Dream: a strong, capable immigrant coming out on top. But I saw the movie as a sort of metaphor for my own life. Mamaw was my keeper, my protector, and, if need be, my own goddamned terminator. No matter what life threw at me, I'd be okay because she was there to protect me.

Paying for her health insurance made me feel, for the first time in my life, like I was the protector. It gave me a sense of satisfaction that I'd never imagined—and how could I? I'd never had the money to help people before the Marines. When I came home, I was able to take Mom out to lunch, get ice cream for the kids, and buy nice Christmas presents for Lindsay. On one of my trips home, Mamaw and I took Lindsay's two oldest kids on a trip to Hocking Hills State Park, a beautiful region of Appalachian Ohio, to meet up with Aunt Wee and Dan. I drove the whole way, I paid for gas, and I bought everyone dinner (admittedly at Wendy's). I felt like such a man, a real grown-up. To laugh and joke with the people I loved most as they scarfed down the meal that I'd provided gave me a feeling of joy and accomplishment that words can't possibly describe.

For my entire life, I had oscillated between fear at my worst moments and a sense of safety and stability at my best. I was either being chased by the bad terminator or protected by the good one. But I had never felt empowered—never believed that I had the ability and the responsibility to care for those I loved. Mamaw could preach about responsibility and hard work, about making something of myself and not making excuses. No pep talk or speech could show me how it felt to transition from seeking shelter to providing it. I had to learn that for myself, and once I did, there was no going back.

Mamaw's seventy-second birthday was in April 2005. Just a couple of weeks before then, I stood in the waiting room of a Walmart Supercenter as car technicians changed my oil. I called

Mamaw on the cell phone that I paid for myself, and she told me about babysitting Lindsay's kids that day. "Meghan is so damned cute," she told me. "I told her to shit in the pot, and for three hours she just kept on saying 'shit in the pot, shit in the pot, shit in the pot' over and over again. I told her she had to stop or I'd get in trouble, but she never did." I laughed, told Mamaw that I loved her, and let her know that her monthly three-hundred-dollar check was on the way. "J.D., thank you for helping me. I'm very proud of you, and I love you."

Two days later I awoke on a Sunday morning to a call from my sister, who said that Mamaw's lung had collapsed, that she was lying in the hospital in a coma, and that I should come home as quickly as possible. Two hours later, I was on the road. I packed my dress blue uniform, just in case I needed it for a funeral. On the way, a West Virginia police officer pulled me over for going ninety-four miles an hour on I–77. He asked why I was in such a hurry, and when I explained, he told me that the highway was clear of speed traps for the next seventy miles, after which I'd cross into Ohio, and that I should go as fast as I wanted until then. I took my warning ticket, thanked him profusely, and drove 102 until I crossed the state line. I made the thirteen-hour trip in just under eleven hours.

When I arrived at Middletown Regional Hospital at eleven in the evening, my entire family was gathered around Mamaw's bed. She was unresponsive, and though her lung had been reinflated, the infection that had caused it to collapse showed no signs of responding to treatment. Until that happened, the doctor told us, it would be torture to wake her—if she could be awakened at all.

We waited a few days for signs that the infection was surrendering to the medication. But the signs showed the opposite: Her white blood cell count continued to rise, and some of her organs showed evidence of severe stress. Her doctor explained that she had no realistic chance of living without a ventilator and feeding tube. We all conferred and decided that if, after a day, Mamaw's white blood cell count increased further, we would pull the plug. Legally, it was Aunt Wee's sole decision, and I'll never forget when she tearfully asked whether I thought she was making a mistake. To this day, I'm convinced that she—and we—made the right decision. I guess it's impossible to know for sure. I wished at the time that we had a doctor in the family.

The doctor told us that without the ventilator Mamaw would die within fifteen minutes, an hour at most. She lasted instead for three hours, fighting to the very last minute. Everyone was present—Uncle Jimmy, Mom, and Aunt Wee; Lindsay, Kevin, and I—and we gathered around her bed, taking turns whispering in her ear and hoping that she heard us. As her heart rate dropped and we realized that her time drew near, I opened a Gideon's Bible to a random passage and began to read. It was First Corinthians, Chapter 13, Verse 12: "For now we see through a glass, darkly; but then face to face: now I know in part; but then shall I know even as also I am known." A few minutes later, she was dead.

I didn't cry when Mamaw died, and I didn't cry for days thereafter. Aunt Wee and Lindsay grew frustrated with me, then worried: You're just so stoic, they said. You need to grieve like the rest of us or you'll burst.

I was grieving in my own way, but I sensed that our entire family was on the verge of collapse, and I wanted to give the impression of emotional strength. We all knew how Mom had reacted to Papaw's death, but Mamaw's death created new pressures: It was time to wind down the estate, figure out Mamaw's debts, dispose of her property, and disburse what remained. For the first time, Uncle Jimmy learned Mom's true financial impact on Mamaw—the drug rehab charges, the numerous "loans" never repaid. To this day, he refuses to speak to her.

For those of us well acquainted with Mamaw's generosity, her financial position came as no surprise. Though Papaw had worked and saved for over four decades, the only thing of value that remained was the house he and Mamaw had purchased fifty years earlier. And Mamaw's debts were large enough to eat into a substantial portion of the home's equity. Lucky for us, this was 2005—the height of the real estate bubble. If she had died in 2008, Mamaw's estate likely would have been bankrupt.

In her will, Mamaw divided what remained between her three kids, with a twist: Mom's share was divided evenly between me and Lindsay. This undoubtedly contributed to Mom's inevitable emotional outburst. I was so caught up in the financial aspects of Mamaw's death and spending time with relatives I hadn't seen in months that I didn't realize Mom was slowly descending to the same place she'd traveled after Papaw's death. But it's hard to miss a freight train barreling down on you, so I noticed soon enough.

Like Papaw, Mamaw wanted a visitation in Middletown so that all of her friends from Ohio could gather and pay their respects. Like Papaw, she wanted a second visitation and funeral back home in Jackson, at Deaton's. After her funeral, the convoy departed for Keck, a holler not far from where Mamaw was born that housed our family's cemetery. In family lore, Keck held an even higher place of honor than Mamaw's birthplace. Her own mother—our beloved Mamaw Blanton—was born in Keck, and

Mamaw Blanton's younger sister—Aunt Bonnie, nearly ninety herself—owned a beautiful log cabin on the same property. A short hike up the mountain from that log cabin is a relatively flat plot of land that serves as the final resting place for Papaw and Mamaw Blanton and a host of relatives, some born in the nineteenth century. That's where our convoy was headed, through the narrow mountain roads, to deliver Mamaw to the family who'd crossed over before her.

I've made that drive with a funeral convoy probably half a dozen times, and every turn reveals a landscape that inspires some memory of fonder times. It's impossible to sit in the car for the twenty-minute trip and not trade stories about the departed, all of which start out "Do you remember that time . . . ?" But after Mamaw's funeral, we didn't recall a series of fond memories about Mamaw and Papaw and Uncle Red and Teaberry and that time Uncle David drove off the side of the mountain, rolled a hundred yards down the hill, and walked away without a scratch. Lindsay and I instead listened to Mom tell us that we were *too sad*, that we loved Mamaw *too much*, and that Mom had the greater right to grief because, in her words, "She was my mom, not yours!"

I have never felt angrier at anyone for anything. For years, I had made excuses for Mom. I had tried to help manage her drug problem, read those stupid books about addiction, and accompanied her to N.A. meetings. I had endured, never complaining, a parade of father figures, all of whom left me feeling empty and mistrustful of men. I had agreed to ride in that car with her on the day she threatened to kill me, and then I had stood before a judge and lied to him to keep her out of jail. I had moved in with her and Matt, and then her and Ken, because I wanted her to get better and thought that if I played along, there was a chance she would. For years, Lindsay called me the "forgiving child"—the one who found the best in Mom, the one who made excuses, the one who believed. I opened my mouth to spew pure vitriol in Mom's direction, but Lindsay spoke first: "No, Mom. She was our mom, too." That said it all, so I continued to sit in silence.

The day after the funeral, I drove back to North Carolina to rejoin my Marine Corps unit. On the way back, on a narrow mountain back road in Virginia, I hit a wet patch of road coming around a turn, and the car began spinning out of control. I was moving fast, and my twisting car showed no signs of slowing as it hurtled towards the guardrail. I thought briefly that this was it—that I'd topple over that guardrail and join Mamaw just a bit sooner than I expected—when all of a sudden the car stopped. It is the closest I've ever come to a true supernatural event, and though I'm sure some law of friction can explain what happened, I imagined that Mamaw had stopped the car from toppling over the side of the mountain. I reoriented the car, returned to my lane, and then pulled off to the side. That was when I broke down and released the tears that I'd held back during the previous two weeks. I spoke to Lindsay and Aunt Wee before restarting my journey, and within a few hours I was back at the base.

My final two years in the Marines flew by and were largely uneventful, though two incidents stand out, each of which speaks to the way the Marine Corps changed my perspective. The first was a moment in time in Iraq, where I was lucky to escape any real fighting but which affected me deeply nonetheless. As a public affairs marine, I would attach to different units to get a sense of their daily routine. Sometimes I'd escort civilian press, but generally I'd take photos or write short stories about individual marines or their work. Early in my deployment, I attached to a civil affairs unit to do community outreach. Civil affairs missions were typically considered more dangerous, as a small number of marines would venture into unprotected Iraqi territory to meet with locals. On our particular mission, senior marines met with local school officials while the rest of us provided security or hung out with the schoolkids, playing soccer and passing out candy and school supplies. One very shy boy approached me and held out his hand. When I gave him a small eraser, his face briefly lit up with joy before he ran away to his family, holding his two-cent prize aloft in triumph. I have never seen such excitement on a child's face.

I don't believe in epiphanies. I don't believe in transformative moments, as transformation is harder than a moment. I've seen far too many people awash in a genuine desire to change only to lose their mettle when they realized just how difficult change actually is. But that moment, with that boy, was pretty close for me. For my entire life, I'd harbored resentment at the world. I was mad at my mother and father, mad that I rode the bus to school while other kids caught rides with friends, mad that my clothes didn't come from Abercrombie, mad that my grandfather died, mad that we lived in a small house. That resentment didn't vanish in an instant, but as I stood and surveyed the mass of children of a war-torn nation, their school without running water, and the overjoyed boy, I began to appreciate how lucky I was: born in the greatest country on earth, every modern convenience at my fingertips, supported by two loving hillbillies, and part of a family that, for all its quirks, loved me unconditionally. At that moment, I resolved to be the type of man who would smile when someone gave him an eraser. I haven't quite made it there, but without that day in Iraq, I wouldn't be trying.

The other life-altering component of my Marine Corps experience was constant. From the first day, with that scary drill instructor and a piece of cake, until the last, when I grabbed my discharge papers and sped home, the Marine Corps taught me how to live like an adult.

The Marine Corps assumes maximum ignorance from its enlisted folks. It assumes that no one taught you anything about physical fitness, personal hygiene, or personal finances. I took mandatory classes about balancing a checkbook, saving, and investing. When I came home from boot camp with my fifteen-hundred-dollar earnings deposited in a mediocre regional bank, a senior enlisted marine drove me to Navy Federal—a respected credit union—and had me open an account. When I caught strep throat and tried to tough it out, my commanding officer noticed and ordered me to the doctor.

We used to complain constantly about the biggest perceived difference between our jobs and civilian jobs: In the civilian world, your boss wasn't able to control your life after you left work. In the Marines, my boss didn't just make sure I did a good job, he made sure I kept my room clean, kept my hair cut, and ironed my uniforms. He sent an older marine to supervise as I shopped for my first car so that I'd end up with a practical car, like a Toyota or a Honda, not the BMW I wanted. When I nearly agreed to finance that purchase directly through the car dealership with a 21-percent-interest-rate loan, my chaperone blew a gasket and ordered me to call Navy Fed and get a second quote (it was less than half the interest). I had no idea that people did these things. Compare banks? I thought they were all the same. Shop around for a loan? I felt so lucky to even get a loan that I was ready to pull the trigger immediately. The Marine Corps demanded that I think strategically about these decisions, and then it taught me how to do so.

Just as important, the Marines changed the expectations that I had for myself. In boot camp, the thought of climbing the thirty-foot rope inspired terror; by the end of my first year, I could climb the rope using only one arm. Before I enlisted, I had never run a mile continuously. On my last physical fitness test, I ran three of them in nineteen minutes. It was in the Marine Corps where I first ordered grown men to do a job and watched them listen; where I learned that leadership depended far more on earning the respect of your subordinates than on bossing them around; where I discovered how to earn that respect; and where I saw that men and women of different social classes and races could work as a team and bond like family. It was the Marine Corps that first gave me an opportunity to truly fail, made me take that opportunity, and then, when I did fail, gave me another chance anyway.

When you work in public affairs, the most senior marines serve as liaisons with the press. The press is the holy grail of Marine Corps public affairs: the biggest audience and the highest stakes. Our media officer at Cherry Point was a captain who, for reasons I never understood, quickly fell out of favor with the base's senior brass. Though he was a captain—eight pay grades higher than I was—because of the wars in Iraq and Afghanistan, there was no ready replacement when he got the ax. So my boss told me that for the next nine months (until my service ended) I would be the media relations officer for one of the largest military bases on the East Coast.

By then I'd grown accustomed to the sometimes random nature of Marine Corps assignments. This was something else entirely. As a friend joked, I had a face for radio, and I wasn't prepared for live TV interviews about happenings on base. The Marine Corps threw me to the wolves. I struggled a bit at first—allowing some photographers to take photos of a classified aircraft; speaking out of turn at a meeting with senior officers—and I got my ass chewed. My boss, Shawn Haney, explained what I needed to do to correct myself. We discussed how to build relationships with the press, how to stay on message, and how to manage my time. I got better, and when hundreds of thousands flocked to our base for a biannual air show, our media relations worked so well that I earned a commendation medal.

The experience taught me a valuable lesson: that I could do it. I could work twenty-hour days when I had to. I could speak clearly and confidently with TV cameras shoved in my face. I could stand in a room with majors, colonels, and generals and hold my own. I could do a captain's job even when I feared I couldn't.

For all my grandma's efforts, for all of her "You can do anything; don't be like those fuckers who think the deck is stacked against them" diatribes, the message had only partially set in before I enlisted. Surrounding me was another message: that I and the people like me weren't good enough; that the reason Middletown produced zero Ivy League graduates was some genetic or character defect. I couldn't possibly see how destructive that mentality was until I escaped it. The Marine Corps replaced it with something else, something that loathes excuses. "Giving it my all" was a catchphrase, something heard in health or gym class. When I first ran three miles, mildly impressed with my mediocre twenty-five-minute time, a terrifying senior drill instructor greeted me at the finish line: "If you're not puking, you're lazy! Stop being fucking lazy!" He then ordered me to sprint between him and a tree repeatedly. Just as I felt I might pass out, he relented. I was heaving, barely able to catch my breath. "That's how you should feel at the end of every run!" he yelled. In the Marines, giving it your all was a way of life.

I'm not saying ability doesn't matter. It certainly helps. But there's something powerful about realizing that you've undersold yourself—that somehow your mind confused lack of effort for inability. This is why, whenever people ask me what I'd most like to change about the white working class, I say, "The feeling that our choices don't matter." The Marine Corps excised that feeling like a surgeon does a tumor.

A few days after my twenty-third birthday, I hopped into the first major purchase I'd ever made—an old Honda Civic—grabbed my discharge papers, and drove one last time from Cherry Point, North Carolina, to Middletown, Ohio. During my four years in the Marines, I had seen, in Haiti, a level of poverty I never knew existed. I witnessed the fiery aftermath of an airplane crash into a residential neighborhood. I had watched Mamaw die and then gone to war a few months later. I had befriended a former crack dealer who turned out to be the hardest-working marine I knew.

When I joined the Marine Corps, I did so in part because I wasn't ready for adulthood. I didn't know how to balance a checkbook, much less how to complete the financial aid forms for college. Now I knew exactly what I wanted out of my life and how to get there. And in three weeks, I'd start classes at Ohio State.

Chapter 11

I arrived for orientation at Ohio State in early September 2007, and I couldn't have been more excited. I remember every little detail about that day: lunch at Chipotle, the first time Lindsay had ever eaten there; the walk from the orientation building to the south campus house that would soon be my Columbus home; the beautiful weather. I met with a guidance counselor who talked me through my first college schedule, which put me in class only four days per week, never before nine thirty in the morning. After the Marine Corps and its five thirty A.M. wake-ups, I couldn't believe my good fortune.

Ohio State's main campus in Columbus is about a hundred miles away from Middletown, meaning it was close enough for weekend visits to my family. For the first time in a few years, I could drop in on Middletown whenever I felt like it. And while Havelock (the North Carolina city closest to my Marine Corps base) was not too different from Middletown, Columbus felt like an urban paradise. It was (and remains) one of the fastest-growing cities in the country, powered in large part by the bustling university that was now my home. OSU grads were starting businesses, historic buildings were being converted into new restaurants and bars, and even the worst neighborhoods seemed to be undergoing significant revitalization. Not long after I moved to Columbus, one of my best friends began working as the promotions director for a local radio station, so I always knew what was happening around town and always had an in to the city's best events, from local festivals to VIP seating for the annual fireworks show.

In many ways, college was very familiar. I made a lot of new friends, but virtually all of them were from southwest Ohio. My six roommates included five graduates of Middletown High School and one graduate of Edgewood High School in nearby Trenton. They were a little younger (the Marine Corps had aged me past the age of the typical freshman), but I knew most of them from back home. My closest friends had already graduated or were about to, but many stayed in Columbus after graduation. Though I didn't know it, I was witnessing a phenomenon that social scientists call "brain drain"—people who are able to leave struggling cities often do, and when they find a new home with educational and work opportunities, they stay there. Years later, I looked at my wedding party of six groomsmen and realized that every single one of them had, like me, grown up in a small Ohio town before leaving for Ohio State. To a man, all of them had found careers outside of their hometowns, and none of them had any interest in ever going back.

By the time I started at Ohio State, the Marine Corps had instilled in me an incredible sense of invincibility. I'd go to classes, do my homework, study at the library, and make it home in time to drink well past midnight with my buddies, then wake up early to go running. My schedule was intense, but everything that had made me fear the independent college life when I was eighteen felt like a piece of cake now. I had puzzled through those financial aid forms with Mamaw a few years earlier, arguing about whether to list her or Mom as my "parent/guardian." We had worried that unless I somehow obtained and submitted the financial information of Bob Hamel (my legal father), I'd be guilty of fraud. The whole experience had made both of us painfully aware of how unfamiliar we were with the outside world. I had nearly failed out of high school, earning Ds and Fs in English I. Now I paid my own bills and earned As in every class I took at my state's flagship university. I felt completely in control of my destiny in a way that I never had before.

I knew that Ohio State was put-up-or-shut-up time. I had left the Marine Corps not just with a sense that I could do what I wanted but also with the capacity to plan. I wanted to go to law school, and I knew that to go to the best law school, I'd need good grades and to ace the infamous Law School Admissions Test, or LSAT. There was much I didn't know, of course. I couldn't really explain why I wanted to go to law school besides the fact that in Middletown the "rich kids" were born to either doctors or lawyers, and I didn't want to work with blood. I didn't know how much else was out there, but the little knowledge I had at least gave me direction, and that was all I needed.

I loathed debt and the sense of limitation it imposed. Though the GI Bill paid for a significant chunk of my education, and Ohio State charged relatively little to an in-state resident, I still needed to cover about twenty thousand dollars of expenses on my own. I took a job at the Ohio Statehouse, working for a remarkably kind senator from the Cincinnati area named Bob Schuler. He was a good man, and I liked his politics, so when constituents called and complained, I tried to explain his positions. I watched lobbyists come and go and overheard the senator and his staff debate whether a particular bill was good for his constituents, good for his state, or good for both. Observing the political process from the inside made me appreciate it in a way that watching cable news never had. Mamaw had thought all politicians were crooks, but I learned that, no matter their politics, that was largely untrue at the Ohio Statehouse.

After a few months at the Ohio Senate, as my bills piled up and I found fewer and fewer ways to make up the difference between my spending and my income (one can donate plasma only twice per week, I learned), I decided to get another job. One nonprofit advertised a part-time job that paid ten dollars an hour, but when I showed up for the interview in khakis, an ugly lime-green shirt, and Marine Corps combat boots (my only non-sneakers at the time) and saw the interviewer's reaction, I knew that I was out of luck. I barely noticed the rejection email a week later. A local nonprofit did work for abused and neglected children, and they also paid ten dollars an hour, so I went to Target, bought a nicer shirt and a pair of black shoes, and came away with a job offer to be a "consultant." I cared about their mission, and they were great people. I began work immediately.

With two jobs and a full-time class load, my schedule intensified, but I didn't mind. I didn't realize there was anything unusual about my commitments until a professor emailed me about meeting after class to discuss a writing assignment. When I sent him my schedule, he was aghast. He sternly told me that I should focus on my education and not let work distractions stand in my way. I smiled, shook his hand, and said thanks, but I did not heed his advice. I liked staying up late to work on assignments, waking up early after only three or four hours of sleep, and patting myself on the back for being able to do it. After so many years of fearing my own future, of worrying that I'd end up like many of my neighbors or family—addicted to drugs or alcohol, in prison, or with kids I couldn't or wouldn't take care of—I felt an incredible momentum. I knew the statistics. I had read the brochures in the social worker's office when I was a kid. I had recognized the look of pity from the hygienist at the low-income dental clinic. I wasn't supposed to make it, but I was doing just fine on my own.

Did I take it too far? Absolutely. I didn't sleep enough. I drank too much and ate Taco Bell at nearly every meal. A week into what I thought was just a really awful cold, a doctor told me that I had mono. I ignored him and kept on living as though NyQuil and DayQuil were magical elixirs. After a week of this, my urine turned a disgusting brown shade, and my temperature registered 103. I realized I might need to take care of myself, so I downed some Tylenol, drank a couple of beers, and went to sleep.

When Mom found out what was happening, she drove to Columbus and took me to the emergency room. She wasn't perfect, she wasn't even a practicing nurse, but she took it as a point of pride to supervise every interaction we had with the health care system. She asked the right questions, got annoyed with doctors when they didn't answer directly, and made sure I had what I needed. I spent two full days in the hospital as doctors emptied five bags of saline to rehydrate me and discovered that I had contracted a staph infection in addition to the mono, which explained why I grew so sick. The doctors released me to Mom, who wheeled me out of the hospital and took me home to recover.

My illness lasted another few weeks, which, happily, coincided with the break between Ohio State's spring and summer terms. When I was in Middletown, I split time between Aunt Wee's and Mom's; both of them cared for me and treated me like a son. It was my first real introduction to the competing emotional demands of Middletown in a post-Mamaw world: I didn't want to hurt Mom's feelings, but the past had created rifts that would likely never go away. I never confronted these demands head-on. I never explained to Mom that no matter how nice and caring she was at any given time—and while I had mono, she couldn't have been a better mother—I just felt uncomfortable around her. To sleep in her house meant talking to husband number five, a kind man but a stranger who would never be anything to me but the future ex–Mr. Mom. It meant looking at her furniture and remembering the time I hid behind it during one of her fights with Bob. It meant trying to understand how Mom could be such a contradiction—a woman who sat patiently with me at the hospital for days and an addict who would lie to her family to extract money from them a month later.

I knew that my increasingly close relationship with Aunt Wee hurt Mom's feelings. She talked about it all the time. "I'm your mother, not her," she'd repeat. To this day, I often wonder whether, if I'd had the courage as an adult that I'd had as a child, Mom might have gotten better. Addicts are at their weakest during emotionally trying times, and I knew that I had the power to save her from at least some bouts of sadness. But I couldn't do it any longer. I didn't know what had changed, but I wasn't that person anymore. Perhaps it was nothing more than self-preservation. Regardless, I couldn't pretend to feel at home with her.

After a few weeks of mono, I felt well enough to return to Columbus and my classes. I'd lost a lot of weight—twenty pounds over four weeks—but otherwise felt pretty good. With the hospital bills piling up, I got a third job (as an SAT tutor at the Princeton Review), which paid an incredible eighteen dollars an hour. Three jobs were too much, so I dropped the job I loved the most—my work at the Ohio senate—because it paid the least. I needed money and the financial freedom it provided, not rewarding work. That, I told myself, would come later.

Shortly before I left, the Ohio senate debated a measure that would significantly curb payday-lending practices. My senator opposed the bill (one of the few senators to do so), and though he never explained why, I liked to think that maybe he and I had something in common. The senators and policy staff debating the bill had little appreciation for the role of payday lenders in the shadow economy that people like me occupied. To them, payday lenders were predatory sharks, charging high interest rates on loans and exorbitant fees for cashed checks. The sooner they were snuffed out, the better.

To me, payday lenders could solve important financial problems. My credit was awful, thanks to a host of terrible financial decisions (some of which weren't my fault, many of which were), so credit cards weren't a possibility. If I wanted to take a girl out to dinner or needed a book for school and didn't have money in the bank, I didn't have many options. (I probably could have asked my aunt or uncle, but I desperately wanted to do things on my own.) One Friday morning I dropped off my rent check, knowing that if I waited another day, the fifty-dollar late fee would kick in. I didn't have enough money to cover the check, but I'd get paid that day and would be able to deposit the money after work. However, after a long day at the senate, I forgot to grab my paycheck before I left. By the time I realized the mistake, I was already home, and the Statehouse staff had left for the weekend. On that day, a three-day payday loan, with a few dollars of interest, enabled me to avoid a significant overdraft fee. The legislators debating the merits of payday lending didn't mention situations like that. The lesson? Powerful people sometimes do things to help people like me without really understanding people like me.

My second year of college started pretty much as my first year had, with a beautiful day and a lot of excitement. With the new job, I was a bit busier, but I didn't mind the work. What I did mind was the gnawing feeling that, at twenty-four, I was a little too old to be a second-year college student. But with four years in the Marine Corps behind me, more separated me from the other students than age. During an undergraduate seminar in foreign policy, I listened as a nineteen-year-old classmate with a hideous beard spouted off about the Iraq war. He explained that those fighting the war were typically less intelligent than those (like him) who immediately went to college. It showed, he argued, in the wanton way soldiers butchered and disrespected Iraqi civilians. It was an objectively terrible opinion—my friends from the Marine Corps spanned the political spectrum and held nearly every conceivable opinion about the war. Many of my Marine Corps friends were staunch liberals who had no love for our commander in chief—then George W. Bush—and felt that we had sacrificed too much for too little gain. But none of them had ever uttered such unreflective tripe.

As the student prattled on, I thought about the never-ending training on how to respect Iraqi culture—never show anyone the bottom of your foot, never address a woman in traditional Muslim garb without first speaking to a male relative. I thought about the security we provided for Iraqi poll workers, and how we studiously explained the importance of their mission without ever pushing our own political views on them. I thought about listening to a young Iraqi (who couldn't speak a word of English) flawlessly rap every single word of 50 Cent's "In Da Club" and laughing along with him and his friends. I thought about my friends who were covered in third-degree burns, "lucky" to have survived an IED attack in the Al-Qaim region of Iraq. And here was this dipshit in a spotty beard telling our class that we murdered people for sport.

I felt an immediate drive to finish college as quickly as possible. I met with a guidance counselor and plotted my exit—I'd need to take classes during the summer and more than double the full-time course load during some terms. It was, even by my heightened standards, an intense year. During a particularly terrible February, I sat down with my calendar and counted the number of days since I'd slept more than four hours in a day. The tally was thirty-nine. But I continued, and in August 2009, after one year and eleven months at Ohio State, I graduated with a double major, summa cum laude. I tried to skip my graduation ceremony, but my family wouldn't let me. So I sat in an uncomfortable chair for three hours before I walked across the podium and received my college diploma. When Gordon Gee, then president of the Ohio State University, paused for an unusually long photograph with the girl who stood in front of me in line, I extended my hand to his assistant, nonverbally asking for the diploma. She handed it to me, and I stepped behind Dr. Gee and down off the podium. I may have been the only graduating student that day to not shake his hand. *On to the next one,* I thought.

I knew I'd go to law school later the next year (my August graduation precluded a 2009 start to law school), so I moved home to save money. Aunt Wee had taken Mamaw's place as the family matriarch: She put out the fires, hosted family gatherings, and kept us all from breaking apart. She had always provided me with a home base after Mamaw's death, but ten months seemed like an imposition; I didn't like the idea of disrupting her family's routine. But she insisted, "J.D., this is your home now. It's the only place for you to stay."

Those last months living in Middletown were among the happiest of my life. I was finally a college graduate, and I knew that I'd soon accomplish another dream—going to law school. I worked odd jobs to save money and grew closer to my aunt's two daughters. Every day I'd get home from work, dusty and sweaty from manual labor, and sit at the dinner table to hear my teenage cousins talk about their days at school and trials with friends. Sometimes I'd help with homework. On Fridays during Lent, I helped with the fish fries at the local Catholic church. That feeling I had in college—that I had survived decades of chaos and heartbreak and finally come out on the other side—deepened.

The incredible optimism I felt about my own life contrasted starkly with the pessimism of so many of my neighbors. Years of decline in the blue-collar economy manifested themselves in the material prospects of Middletown's residents. The Great Recession, and the not-great recovery that followed, had hastened Middletown's downward trajectory. But there was something almost spiritual about the cynicism of the community at large, something that went much deeper than a short-term recession.

As a culture, we had no heroes. Certainly not any politician—Barack Obama was then the most admired man in America (and likely still is), but even when the country was enraptured by his rise, most Middletonians viewed him suspiciously. George W. Bush had few fans in 2008. Many loved Bill Clinton, but many more saw him as the symbol of American moral decay, and Ronald Reagan was long dead. We loved the military but had no George S. Patton figure in the modern army. I doubt my neighbors could even name a high-ranking military officer. The space program, long a source of pride, had gone the way of the dodo, and with it the celebrity astronauts. Nothing united us with the core fabric of American society. We felt trapped in two seemingly unwinnable wars, in which a disproportionate share of the fighters came from our neighborhood, and in an economy that failed to deliver the most basic promise of the American Dream—a steady wage.

To understand the significance of this cultural detachment, you must appreciate that much of my family's, my neighborhood's, and my community's identity derives from our love of country. I couldn't tell you a single thing about Breathitt County's mayor, its health care services, or its famous residents. But I do know this: "Bloody Breathitt" allegedly earned its name because the county filled its World War I draft quota entirely with volunteers—the only county in the entire United States to do so. Nearly a century later, and that's the factoid about Breathitt that I remember best: It's the truth that everyone around me ensured I knew. I once interviewed Mamaw for a class project about World War II. After seventy years filled with marriage, children, grandchildren, death, poverty, and triumph, the thing about which Mamaw was unquestionably the proudest and most excited was that she and her family did their part during World War II. We spoke for minutes about everything else; we spoke for hours about war rations, Rosie the Riveter, her dad's wartime love letters to her mother from the Pacific, and the day "we dropped the bomb." Mamaw always had two gods: Jesus Christ and the United States of America. I was no different, and neither was anyone else I knew.

I'm the kind of patriot whom people on the Acela corridor laugh at. I choke up when I hear Lee Greenwood's cheesy anthem

"Proud to Be an American." When I was sixteen, I vowed that every time I met a veteran, I would go out of my way to shake his or her hand, even if I had to awkwardly interject to do so. To this day, I refuse to watch *Saving Private Ryan* around anyone but my closest friends, because I can't stop from crying during the final scene.

Mamaw and Papaw taught me that we live in the best and greatest country on earth. This fact gave meaning to my childhood. Whenever times were tough—when I felt overwhelmed by the drama and the tumult of my youth—I knew that better days were ahead because I lived in a country that allowed me to make the good choices that others hadn't. When I think today about my life and how genuinely incredible it is—a gorgeous, kind, brilliant life partner; the financial security that I dreamed about as a child; great friends and exciting new experiences—I feel overwhelming appreciation for these United States. I know it's corny, but it's the way I feel.

If Mamaw's second God was the United States of America, then many people in my community were losing something akin to a religion. The tie that bound them to their neighbors, that inspired them in the way my patriotism had always inspired me, had seemingly vanished.

The symptoms are all around us. Significant percentages of white conservative voters—about one-third—believe that Barack Obama is a Muslim. In one poll, 32 percent of conservatives said that they believed Obama was foreign-born and another 19 percent said they were unsure—which means that a majority of white conservatives aren't certain that Obama is even an American. I regularly hear from acquaintances or distant family members that Obama has ties to Islamic extremists, or is a traitor, or was born in some far-flung corner of the world.

Many of my new friends blame racism for this perception of the president. But the president feels like an alien to many Middletonians for reasons that have nothing to do with skin color. Recall that not a single one of my high school classmates attended an Ivy League school. Barack Obama attended two of them and excelled at both. He is brilliant, wealthy, and speaks like a constitutional law professor—which, of course, he is. Nothing about him bears any resemblance to the people I admired growing up: His accent—clean, perfect, neutral—is foreign; his credentials are so impressive that they're frightening; he made his life in Chicago, a dense metropolis; and he conducts himself with a confidence that comes from knowing that the modern American meritocracy was built for him. Of course, Obama overcame adversity in his own right—adversity familiar to many of us—but that was long before any of us knew him.

President Obama came on the scene right as so many people in my community began to believe that the modern American meritocracy was not built for *them*. We know we're not doing well. We see it every day: in the obituaries for teenage kids that conspicuously omit the cause of death (reading between the lines: overdose), in the deadbeats we watch our daughters waste their time with. Barack Obama strikes at the heart of our deepest insecurities. He is a good father while many of us aren't. He wears suits to his job while we wear overalls, if we're lucky enough to have a job at all. His wife tells us that we shouldn't be feeding our children certain foods, and we hate her for it—not because we think she's wrong but because we know she's right.

Many try to blame the anger and cynicism of working-class whites on misinformation. Admittedly, there is an industry of conspiracy-mongers and fringe lunatics writing about all manner of idiocy, from Obama's alleged religious leanings to his ancestry.

But every major news organization, even the oft-maligned Fox News, has always told the truth about Obama's citizenship status and religious views. The people I know are well aware of what the major news organizations have to say about the issue; they simply don't believe them. Only 6 percent of American voters believe that the media is "very trustworthy."[21] To many of us, the free press—that bulwark of American democracy—is simply full of shit.

With little trust in the press, there's no check on the Internet conspiracy theories that rule the digital world. Barack Obama is a foreign alien actively trying to destroy our country. Everything the media tells us is a lie. Many in the white working class believe the worst about their society. Here's a small sample of emails or messages I've seen from friends or family:

- From right-wing radio talker Alex Jones on the ten-year anniversary of 9/11, a documentary about the "unanswered question" of the terrorist attacks, suggesting that the U.S. government played a role in the massacre of its own people.
- From an email chain, a story that the Obamacare legislation requires microchip implantation in new health care patients. This story carries extra bite because of the religious implications: Many believe that the End Times "mark of the beast" foretold in biblical prophecy will be an electronic device. Multiple friends warned others about this threat via social media.
- From the popular website WorldNetDaily, an editorial suggesting that the Newtown gun massacre was engineered by the federal government to turn public opinion on gun control measures.

- From multiple Internet sources, suggestions that Obama will soon implement martial law in order to secure power for a third presidential term.

The list goes on. It's impossible to know how many people believe one or many of these stories. But if a third of our community questions the president's origin—despite all evidence to the contrary—it's a good bet that the other conspiracies have broader currency than we'd like. This isn't some libertarian mistrust of government policy, which is healthy in any democracy. This is deep skepticism of the very institutions of our society. And it's becoming more and more mainstream.

We can't trust the evening news. We can't trust our politicians. Our universities, the gateway to a better life, are rigged against us. We can't get jobs. You can't believe these things and participate meaningfully in society. Social psychologists have shown that group belief is a powerful motivator in performance. When groups perceive that it's in their interest to work hard and achieve things, members of that group outperform other similarly situated individuals. It's obvious why: If you believe that hard work pays off, then you work hard; if you think it's hard to get ahead even when you try, then why try at all?

Similarly, when people do fail, this mind-set allows them to look outward. I once ran into an old acquaintance at a Middletown bar who told me that he had recently quit his job because he was sick of waking up early. I later saw him complaining on Facebook about the "Obama economy" and how it had affected his life. I don't doubt that the Obama economy has affected many, but this man is assuredly not among them. His status in life is directly attributable to the choices he's made, and his life will improve only through better decisions. But for him to make better choices, he needs to live in an environment that forces him to ask tough questions about himself. There is a cultural movement in the white working class to blame problems on society or the government, and that movement gains adherents by the day.

Here is where the rhetoric of modern conservatives (and I say this as one of them) fails to meet the real challenges of their biggest constituents. Instead of encouraging engagement, conservatives increasingly foment the kind of detachment that has sapped the ambition of so many of my peers. I have watched some friends blossom into successful adults and others fall victim to the worst of Middletown's temptations—premature parenthood, drugs, incarceration. What separates the successful from the unsuccessful are the expectations that they had for their own lives. Yet the message of the right is increasingly: It's not your fault that you're a loser; it's the government's fault.

My dad, for example, has never disparaged hard work, but he mistrusts some of the most obvious paths to upward mobility. When he found out that I had decided to go to Yale Law, he asked whether, on my applications, I had "pretended to be black or liberal." This is how low the cultural expectations of working-class white Americans have fallen. We should hardly be surprised that as attitudes like this one spread, the number of people willing to work for a better life diminishes.

The Pew Economic Mobility Project studied how Americans evaluated their chances at economic betterment, and what they found was shocking. There is no group of Americans more pessimistic than working-class whites. Well over half of blacks, Latinos, and college-educated whites expect that their children will fare better economically than they have. Among working-class whites, only 44 percent share that expectation. Even more surprising, 42 percent of working-class whites—by far the highest number in the survey—report that their lives are less economically successful than those of their parents'.

In 2010, that just wasn't my mind-set. I was happy about where I was and overwhelmingly hopeful about the future. For the first time in my life, I felt like an outsider in Middletown. And what turned me into an alien was my optimism.

Chapter 12

During my first round of law school applications, I didn't even apply to Yale, Harvard, or Stanford—the mythical "top three" schools. I didn't think I had a chance at those places. More important, I didn't think it mattered; all lawyers get good jobs, I assumed. I just needed to get to any law school, and then I'd do fine: a nice salary, a respectable profession, and the American Dream. Then my best friend, Darrell, ran into one of his law school classmates at a popular D.C. restaurant. She was bussing tables, simply because that was the only job available to her. On the next round, I gave Yale and Harvard a try.

I didn't apply to Stanford—one of the very best schools in the country—and to know why is to understand that the lessons I learned as a kid were sometimes counterproductive. Stanford's law school application wasn't the standard combination of college transcript, LSAT score, and essays. It required a personal sign-off from the dean of your college: You had to submit a form, completed by the dean, attesting that you weren't a loser.

I didn't know the dean of my college at Ohio State. It's a big place. I'm sure she is a lovely person, and the form was clearly little more than a formality. But I just couldn't ask. I had never met this person, never taken a class with her, and, most of all, didn't trust her. Whatever virtues she possessed as a person, she was, in the abstract, an outsider. The professors I'd selected to write my letters had gained my trust. I listened to them nearly every day, took their tests, and wrote papers for them. As much as I loved Ohio State and its people for an incredible education and experience, I could not put my fate in the hands of someone I didn't know. I tried to talk myself into it. I even printed the form and drove it to campus. But when the time came, I crumpled it up and tossed it in the garbage. There would be no Stanford Law for J.D.

I decided that I wanted to go to Yale more than any other school. It had a certain aura—with its small class sizes and unique grading system, Yale billed itself as a low-stress way to jump-start a legal career. But most of its students came from elite private colleges, not large state schools like mine, so I imagined that I had no chance of admission. Nonetheless, I submitted an application online, because that was relatively easy. It was late afternoon on an early spring day, 2010, when my phone rang and the caller ID revealed an unfamiliar 203 area code. I answered, and the voice on the other line told me that he was the director of admissions at Yale Law, and that I'd been admitted to the class of 2013. I was ecstatic and leaped around during the entire three-minute conversation. By the time he said goodbye, I was so out of breath that when I called Aunt Wee to tell her, she thought I'd just gotten into a car accident.

I was sufficiently committed to going to Yale Law that I was willing to accept the two hundred thousand dollars or so in debt that I knew I'd accrue. Yet the financial aid package Yale offered exceeded my wildest dreams. In my first year, it was nearly a full ride. That wasn't because of anything I'd done or earned—it was because I was one of the poorest kids in school. Yale offered tens of thousands in need-based aid. It was the first time being so broke paid so well. Yale wasn't just my dream school, it was also the cheapest option on the table.

The New York Times recently reported that the most expensive schools are paradoxically cheaper for low-income students. Take, for example, a student whose parents earn thirty thousand per year—not a lot of money but not poverty level, either. That student would pay ten thousand for one of the less selective branch campuses of the University of Wisconsin but would pay six thousand at the school's flagship Madison campus. At Harvard, the student would pay only about thirteen hundred despite tuition of over forty thousand. Of course, kids like me don't know this. My buddy Nate, a lifelong friend and one of the smartest people I know, wanted to go to the University of Chicago as an undergraduate, but he didn't apply because he knew he couldn't afford it. It likely would have cost him considerably less than Ohio State, just as Yale cost considerably less for me than any other school.

I spent the next few months getting ready to leave. My aunt and uncle's friend got me that job at a local floor tile distribution warehouse, and I worked there during the summer—driving a forklift, getting tile shipments ready for transport, and sweeping a giant warehouse. By the end of the summer, I'd saved enough not to worry about the move to New Haven.

The day I moved felt different from every other time I'd moved away from Middletown. I knew when I left for the Marines that I'd return often and that life might bring me back to my hometown for an extended period (indeed it did). After four years in the Marines, the move to Columbus for college hadn't seemed all that significant. I'd become an expert at leaving Middletown for other places, and each time I felt at least a little forlorn. But I knew this time that I was never really coming back. That didn't bother me. Middletown no longer felt like home.

On my first day at Yale Law School, there were posters in the hallways announcing an event with Tony Blair, the former British prime minister. I couldn't believe it: Tony Blair was speaking to a room of a few dozen students? If he came to Ohio State, he would have filled an auditorium of a thousand people. "Yeah, he speaks at Yale all the time," a friend told me. "His son is an undergraduate." A few days after that, I nearly bumped into a man as I turned a corner to walk into the law school's main entrance. I said, "Excuse me," looked up, and realized the man was New York governor George Pataki. These sorts of things happened at least once a week. Yale Law School was like nerd Hollywood, and I never stopped feeling like an awestruck tourist.

The first semester was structured in a way to make life easy on students. While my friends in other law schools were overwhelmed with work and worrying about strict grading curves that effectively placed you in direct competition with your classmates, our dean asked us during orientation to follow our passions, wherever they might lead, and not worry so much about grades. Our first four classes were graded on a credit/no credit basis, which made that easy. One of those classes, a constitutional law seminar of sixteen students, became a kind of family for me. We called ourselves the island of misfit toys, as there was no real unifying force to our team—a conservative hillbilly from Appalachia, the supersmart daughter of Indian immigrants, a black

Canadian with decades' worth of street smarts, a neuroscientist from Phoenix, an aspiring civil rights attorney born a few minutes from Yale's campus, and an extremely progressive lesbian with a fantastic sense of humor, among others—but we became excellent friends.

That first year at Yale was overwhelming, but in a good way. I'd always been an American history buff, and some of the buildings on campus predated the Revolutionary War. Sometimes I'd walk around campus searching for the placards that identified the ages of buildings. The buildings themselves were breathtakingly beautiful—towering masterpieces of neo-Gothic architecture. Inside, intricate stone carvings and wood trim gave the law school an almost medieval feel. You'd even sometimes hear that we went to HLS (Hogwarts Law School). It's telling that the best way to describe the law school was a reference to a series of fantasy novels.

Classes were hard, and sometimes required long nights in the library, but they weren't *that* hard. A part of me had thought I'd finally be revealed as an intellectual fraud, that the administration would realize they'd made a terrible mistake and send me back to Middletown with their sincerest apologies. Another part of me thought I'd be able to hack it but only with extraordinary dedication; after all, these were the brightest students in the world, and I did not qualify as such. But that didn't end up being the case. Though there were rare geniuses walking the halls of the law school, most of my fellow students were smart but not intimidatingly so. In classroom discussions and on tests, I largely held my own.

Not everything came easy. I always fancied myself a decent writer, but when I turned in a sloppy writing assignment to a famously stern professor, he handed it back with some extraordinarily critical commentary. "Not good at all," he scribbled on one page. On another, he circled a large paragraph and wrote in the margin, "This is a vomit of sentences masquerading as a paragraph. Fix." I heard through the grapevine that this professor thought Yale should accept only students from places like Harvard, Yale, Stanford, and Princeton: "It's not our job to do remedial education, and too many of these other kids need it." That committed me to changing his mind. By the end of the semester, he called my writing "excellent" and admitted that he might have been wrong about state schools. As the first year drew to a close, I felt triumphant—my professors and I got along well, I had earned solid grades, and I had a dream job for the summer—working for the chief counsel for a sitting U.S. senator.

Yet, for all of the joy and intrigue, Yale planted a seed of doubt in my mind about whether I belonged. This place was so beyond the pale for what I expected of myself. I knew zero Ivy League graduates back home; I was the first person in my nuclear family to go to college and the first person in my extended family to attend a professional school. When I arrived in August 2010, Yale had educated two of the three most recent Supreme Court justices and two of the six most recent presidents, not to mention the sitting secretary of state (Hillary Clinton). There was something bizarre about Yale's social rituals: the cocktail receptions and banquets that served as both professional networking and personal matchmaking events. I lived among newly christened members of what folks back home pejoratively call the "elites," and by every outward appearance, I was one of them: I am a tall, white, straight male. I have never felt out of place in my entire life. But I did at Yale.

Part of it has to do with social class. A student survey found that over 95 percent of Yale Law's students qualified as upper-middle-class or higher, and most of them qualified as outright wealthy. Obviously, I was neither upper-middle-class nor wealthy. Very few people at Yale Law School are like me. They may look like me, but for all of the Ivy League's obsession with diversity, virtually everyone—black, white, Jewish, Muslim, whatever—comes from intact families who never worry about money. Early during my first year, after a late night of drinking with my classmates, we all decided to stop at a New Haven chicken joint. Our large group left an awful mess: dirty plates, chicken bones, ranch dressing and soda splattered on the tables, and so on. I couldn't imagine leaving it all for some poor guy to clean up, so I stayed behind. Of a dozen classmates, only one person helped me: my buddy Jamil, who also came from a poorer background. Afterward, I told Jamil that we were probably the only people in the school who'd ever had to clean up someone else's mess. He just nodded his head in silent agreement.

Even though my experiences were unique, I never felt like a foreigner in Middletown. Most people's parents had never gone to college. My closest friends had all seen some kind of domestic strife in their life—divorces, remarriages, legal separations, or fathers who spent some time in jail. A few parents worked as lawyers, engineers, or teachers. They were "rich people" to Mamaw, but they were never so rich that I thought of them as fundamentally different. They still lived within walking distance of my house, sent their kids to the same high school, and generally did the same things the rest of us did. It never occurred to me that I didn't belong, even in the homes of some of my relatively wealthy friends.

At Yale Law School, I felt like my spaceship had crashed in Oz. People would say with a straight face that a surgeon mother and engineer father were middle-class. In Middletown, $160,000 is an unfathomable salary; at Yale Law School, students expect to earn that amount in the first year after law school. Many of them are already worried that it won't be enough.

It wasn't just about the money or my relative lack of it. It was about people's perceptions. Yale made me feel, for the first time in my life, that others viewed my life with intrigue. Professors and classmates seemed genuinely interested in what seemed to me a superficially boring story: I went to a mediocre public high school, my parents didn't go to college, and I grew up in Ohio. The same was true of nearly everyone I knew. At Yale, these things were true of no one. Even my service in the Marine Corps was pretty common in Ohio, but at Yale, many of my friends had never spent time with a veteran of America's newest wars. In other words, I was an anomaly.

That's not exactly a bad thing. For much of that first year in law school, I reveled in the fact that I was the only big marine with a Southern twang at my elite law school. But as law school acquaintances became close friends, I became less comfortable with the lies I told about my own past. "My mom is a nurse," I told them. But of course that wasn't true anymore. I didn't really know what my legal father—the one whose name was on my birth certificate—did for a living; he was a total stranger. No one, except my best friends from Middletown whom I asked to read my law school admissions essay, knew about the formative experiences that shaped my life. At Yale, I decided to change that.

I'm not sure what motivated this change. Part of it is that I stopped being ashamed: My parents' mistakes were not my fault, so I had no reason to hide them. But I was concerned most of all that no one understood my grandparents' outsize role in my life. Few of even my closest friends understood how utterly hopeless my life would have been without Mamaw and Papaw. So maybe I just wanted to give credit where credit is due.

Yet there's something else. As I realized how different I was from my classmates at Yale, I grew to appreciate how similar I was to the people back home. Most important, I became acutely aware of the inner conflict born of my recent success. On one of my first visits home after classes began, I stopped at a gas station not far from Aunt Wee's house. The woman at the nearest pump began a conversation, and I noticed that she wore a Yale T-shirt. "Did you go to Yale?" I asked. "No," she replied, "but my nephew does. Do you?" I wasn't sure what to say. It was stupid—her nephew went to school there, for Christ's sake—but I was still uncomfortable admitting that I'd become an Ivy Leaguer. The moment she told me her nephew went to Yale, I had to choose: Was I a Yale Law student, or was I a Middletown kid with hillbilly grandparents? If the former, I could exchange pleasantries and talk about New Haven's beauty; if the latter, she occupied the other side of an invisible divide and could not to be trusted. At her cocktail parties and fancy dinners, she and her nephew probably even laughed about the unsophisticates of Ohio and how they clung to their guns and religion. I would not join forces with her. My answer was a pathetic attempt at cultural defiance: "No, I don't go to Yale. But my girlfriend does." And then I got in my car and drove away.

This wasn't one of my prouder moments, but it highlights the inner conflict inspired by rapid upward mobility: I had lied to a stranger to avoid feeling like a traitor. There are lessons to draw here, among them what I've noted already: that one consequence of isolation is seeing standard metrics of success as not just un-attainable but as the property of people not like us. Mamaw always fought that attitude in me, and for the most part, she was successful.

Another lesson is that it's not just our own communities that reinforce the outsider attitude, it's the places and people that upward mobility connects us with—like my professor who suggested that Yale Law School shouldn't accept applicants from non-prestigious state schools. There's no way to quantify how these attitudes affect the working class. We do know that working-class Americans aren't just less likely to climb the eco-nomic ladder, they're also more likely to fall off even after they've reached the top. I imagine that the discomfort they feel at leaving behind much of their identity plays at least a small role in this problem. One way our upper class can promote upward mobility, then, is not only by pushing wise public policies but by opening their hearts and minds to the newcomers who don't quite belong.

Though we sing the praises of social mobility, it has its down-sides. The term necessarily implies a sort of movement—to a theoretically better life, yes, but also away from something. And you can't always control the parts of your old life from which you drift. In the past few years, I've vacationed in Panama and England. I've bought my groceries at Whole Foods. I've watched orchestral concerts. I've tried to break my addiction to "refined processed sugars" (a term that includes at least one too many words). I've worried about racial prejudice in my own family and friends.

None of these things is bad on its own. In fact, most of them are good—visiting England was a childhood dream; eating less sugar improves health. At the same time, they've shown me that social mobility isn't just about money and economics, it's about a lifestyle change. The wealthy and the powerful aren't just wealthy and powerful; they follow a different set of norms and mores. When you go from working-class to professional-class, almost everything about your old life becomes unfashionable at best or unhealthy at worst. At no time was this more obvious than the first (and last) time I took a Yale friend to Cracker Barrel. In my youth, it was the height of fine dining—my grandma's and my favorite restaurant. With Yale friends, it was a greasy public health crisis.

These aren't exactly major problems, and if given the option all over again, I'd trade a bit of social discomfort for the life I lead in a heartbeat. But as I realized that in this new world I was the cultural alien, I began to think seriously about questions that had nagged at me since I was a teenager: Why has no one else from my high school made it to the Ivy League? Why are people like me so poorly represented in America's elite institutions? Why is domestic strife so common in families like mine? Why did I think that places like Yale and Harvard were so unreachable? Why did successful people feel so *different*?

Chapter 13

As I began to think a bit more deeply about my own identity, I fell hard for a classmate of mine named Usha. As luck would have it, we were assigned as partners for our first major writing assignment, so we spent a lot of time during that first year getting to know each other. She seemed some sort of genetic anomaly, a combination of every positive quality a human being should have: bright, hardworking, tall, and beautiful. I joked with a buddy that if she had possessed a terrible personality, she would have made an excellent heroine in an Ayn Rand novel, but she had a great sense of humor and an extraordinarily direct way of speaking. Where others might have asked meekly, "Yeah, maybe you could rephrase this?" or "Have you thought about this other idea?" Usha would say simply: "I think this sentence needs work" or "This is a pretty terrible argument." At a bar, she looked up at a mutual friend of ours and said, without a hint of irony, "You have a very small head." I had never met anyone like her.

I had dated other girls before, some serious, some not. But Usha occupied an entirely different emotional universe. I thought about her constantly. One friend described me as "heartsick" and another told me he had never seen me like this. Toward the end of our first year, I learned that Usha was single, and I immediately asked her out. After a few weeks of flirtations and a single date, I told her that I was in love with her. It violated every rule of modern dating I'd learned as a young man, but I didn't care.

Usha was like my Yale spirit guide. She'd attended the university for college, too, and knew all of the best coffee shops and places to eat. Her knowledge went much deeper, however: She instinctively understood the questions I didn't even know to ask, and she always encouraged me to seek opportunities that I didn't know existed. "Go to office hours," she'd tell me. "Professors here like to engage with students. It's part of the experience here." In a place that always seemed a little foreign, Usha's presence made me feel at home.

I went to Yale to earn a law degree. But that first year at Yale taught me most of all that I didn't know how the world worked. Every August, recruiters from prestigious law firms descend on New Haven, hungry for the next generation of high-quality legal talent. The students call it FIP—short for Fall Interview Program—and it's a marathon week of dinners, cocktail hours, hospitality suite visits, and interviews. On my first day of FIP, just before second-year classes began, I had six interviews, including one with the firm I most coveted—Gibson, Dunn & Crutcher, LLP (Gibson Dunn for short)—which had an elite practice in Washington, D.C.

The interview with Gibson Dunn went well and I was invited to their infamous dinner at one of New Haven's fanciest restaurants. The rumor mill informed me that the dinner was a kind of intermediate interview: We needed to be funny, charming, and engaging, or we'd never be invited to the D.C. or New York offices for final interviews. When I arrived at the restaurant, I thought it a pity that the most expensive meal I'd ever eaten would take place in such a high-stakes environment.

Before dinner, we were all corralled into a private banquet room for wine and conversation. Women a decade older than I was carried around wine bottles wrapped in beautiful linens, asking every few minutes whether I wanted a new glass of wine or a refill on the old one. At first I was too nervous to drink. But I finally mustered the courage to answer yes when someone asked whether I'd like some wine and, if so, what kind. "I'll take white," I said, which I thought would settle the matter. "Would you like sauvignon blanc or chardonnay?"

I thought she was screwing with me. But I used my powers of deduction to determine that those were two separate *kinds* of white wine. So I ordered a chardonnay, not because I didn't know what sauvignon blanc was (though I didn't) but because it was easier to pronounce. I had just dodged my first bullet. The night, however, was young.

At these types of events, you have to strike a balance between shy and overbearing. You don't want to annoy the partners, but you don't want them to leave without shaking your hand. I tried to be myself; I've always considered myself gregarious but not op-pressive. But I was so impressed by the environment that "being myself" meant staring slack-jawed at the fineries of the restau-rant and wondering how much they cost.

The wineglasses look like they've been Windexed. That dude did not buy his suit at the three-suits-for-one sale at Jos. A. Bank; it looks like it's made from silk. The linens on the table look softer than my bedsheets; I need to touch them without being weird about it. Long story short,

I needed a new plan. By the time we sat down for dinner, I'd resolved to focus on the task at hand—getting a job—and leave the class tourism for later.

My bearing lasted another two minutes. After we sat down, the waitress asked whether I'd like tap or sparkling water. I rolled my eyes at that one: As impressed as I was with the restaurant, calling the water "sparkling" was just *too* pretentious—like "sparkling" crystal or a "sparkling" diamond. But I ordered the sparkling water anyway. Probably better for me. Fewer contaminants.

I took one sip and literally spit it out. It was the grossest thing I'd ever tasted. I remember once getting a Diet Coke at a Subway without realizing that the fountain machine didn't have enough Diet Coke syrup. That's exactly what this fancy place's "sparkling" water tasted like. "Something's wrong with that water," I protested. The waitress apologized and told me she'd get me another Pellegrino. That was when I realized that "sparkling" water meant "carbonated" water. I was mortified, but luckily only one other person noticed what had happened, and she was a classmate. I was in the clear. No more mistakes.

Immediately thereafter, I looked down at the place setting and observed an absurd number of instruments. Nine utensils? Why, I wondered, did I need three spoons? Why were there multiple butter knives? Then I recalled a scene from a movie and realized there was some social convention surrounding the placement and size of the cutlery. I excused myself to the restroom and called my spirit guide: "What do I do with all these damned forks? I don't want to make a fool of myself." Armed with Usha's reply— "Go from outside to inside, and don't use the same utensil for separate dishes; oh, and use the fat spoon for soup"—I returned to dinner, ready to dazzle my future employers.

The rest of the evening was uneventful. I chatted politely and remembered Lindsay's admonition to chew with my mouth closed. Those at our table talked about law and law school, firm culture, and even a little politics. The recruiters we ate with were very nice, and everyone at my table landed a job offer—even the guy who spit out his sparkling water.

It was at this meal, on the first of five grueling days of interviews, that I began to understand that I was seeing the inner workings of a system that lay hidden to most of my kind. Our career office had emphasized the importance of sounding natural and being someone the interviewers wouldn't mind sitting with on an airplane. It made perfect sense—after all, who wants to work with an asshole?—but it seemed an odd emphasis for what felt like the most important moment of a young career. Our interviews weren't so much about grades or résumés, we were told; thanks to a Yale Law pedigree, one foot was already in the door. The interviews were about passing a social test—a test of belonging, of holding your own in a corporate boardroom, of making connections with potential future clients.

The most difficult test was the one I wasn't even required to take: getting an audience in the first place. All week I marveled at the ease of access to the most esteemed lawyers in the country. All of my friends had at least a dozen interviews, and most led to job offers. I had sixteen when the week began, though by the end I was so spoiled (and exhausted) by the process that I turned down a couple of interviews. Two years earlier, I had applied to dozens of places in the hope of landing a well-paying job after college but was rebuffed every time. Now, after only a year at Yale Law, my classmates and I were being handed six-figure salaries by men who had argued before the United States Supreme Court.

It was pretty clear that there was some mysterious force at work, and I had just tapped into it for the first time. I had always thought that when you need a job, you look online for job postings. And then you submit a dozen résumés. And then you hope that someone calls you back. If you're lucky, maybe a friend puts your résumé at the top of the pile. If you're qualified for a very high-demand profession, like accounting, maybe the job search comes a bit easier. But the rules are basically the same.

The problem is, virtually everyone who plays by those rules fails. That week of interviews showed me that successful people are playing an entirely different game. They don't flood the job market with résumés, hoping that some employer will grace them with an interview. They network. They email a friend of a friend to make sure their name gets the look it deserves. They have their uncles call old college buddies. They have their school's career service office set up interviews months in advance on their behalf. They have parents tell them how to dress, what to say, and whom to schmooze.

That doesn't mean the strength of your résumé or interview performance is irrelevant. Those things certainly matter. But there is enormous value in what economists call social capital. It's a professor's term, but the concept is pretty simple: The networks of people and institutions around us have real economic value. They connect us to the right people, ensure that we have opportunities, and impart valuable information. Without them, we're going it alone.

I learned this the hard way during one of my final interviews of the marathon FIP week. At that point, the interviews were like a broken record. People asked about my interests, my favorite classes, my expected legal specialty. Then they asked if I had any questions. After a dozen tries, my answers were polished, and my questions made me sound like a seasoned consumer of law firm information. The truth was that I had no idea what I wanted to do and no idea what field of law I expected to practice in. I wasn't even sure what my questions about "firm culture" and "work-life balance" meant. The whole process was little more than a dog and pony show. But I didn't seem like an asshole, so I was coasting.

Then I hit a wall. The last interviewer asked me a question I was unprepared to answer: Why did I want to work for a law firm? It was a softball, but I'd gotten so used to talking about my budding interest in antitrust litigation (an interest that was at least a little fabricated) that I was laughably unprepared. I should have said something about learning from the best or working on high-stakes litigation. I should have said anything other than what came from my mouth: "I don't really know, but the pay isn't bad! Ha ha!" The interviewer looked at me like I had three eyes, and the conversation never recovered.

I was certain I was toast. I had flubbed the interview in the worst way. But behind the scenes, one of my recommenders was already working the phones. She told the hiring partner that I was a smart, good kid and would make an excellent lawyer. "She raved about you," I later heard. So when the recruiters called to schedule the next round of interviews, I made the cut. I eventually got the job, despite failing miserably at what I perceived was the most important part of the recruiting process. The old adage says that it's better to be lucky than good. Apparently having the right network is better than both.

At Yale, networking power is like the air we breathe—so pervasive that it's easy to miss. Toward the end of our first year, most of us were studying for *The Yale Law Journal* writing competition. The *Journal* publishes lengthy pieces of legal analysis, mostly for an academic audience. The articles read like radiator manuals—dry, formulaic, and partially written in another language. (A sampling: "Despite grading's great promise, we show that the regulatory design, implementation, and practice suffer from serious flaws: jurisdictions fudge more than nudge.") Kidding aside, *Journal* membership is serious business. It is the single most significant extracurricular activity for legal employers, some of whom hire only from the publication's editorial board.

Some kids came to the law school with a plan for admission to *The Yale Law Journal*. The writing competition kicked off in April. By March, some people were weeks into preparation. On the advice of recent graduates (who were also close friends), a good friend had begun studying before Christmas. The alumni of elite consulting firms gathered together to grill each other on editorial techniques. One second-year student helped his old Harvard roommate (a first-year student) design a study strategy for the final month before the test. At every turn, people were tapping into friendship circles and alumni groups to learn about the most important test of our first year.

I had no idea what was going on. There was no Ohio State alumni group—when I arrived, I was one of two Ohio State graduates at the entire law school. I suspected the *Journal* was important, because Supreme Court justice Sonia Sotomayor had been a member. But I didn't know why. I didn't even know what the *Journal* did. The entire process was a black box, and no one I knew had the key.

There were official channels of information. But they telegraphed conflicting messages. Yale prides itself on being a low-stress, noncompetitive law school. Unfortunately, that ethos sometimes manifests itself in confused messaging. No one seemed to know what value the credential actually held. We were told that the *Journal* was a huge career boost but that it wasn't that important, that we shouldn't stress about it but that it was a prerequisite for certain types of jobs. This was undoubtedly true: For many career paths and interests, *Journal* membership was merely wasted time. But I didn't know *which* career paths that applied to. And I was unsure how to find out.

It was around this time that Amy Chua, one of my professors, stepped in and told me exactly how things worked: "*Journal* membership is useful if you want to work for a judge or if you want to be an academic. Otherwise, it's a waste. But if you're unsure what you want to do, go ahead and try out." It was million-dollar advice. Because I was unsure what I wanted, I followed it. Though I didn't make it during my first year, I made the cut during my second year and became an editor of the prestigious publication. Whether I made it isn't the point. What mattered was that, with a professor's help, I had closed the information gap. It was like I'd learned to see.

This wasn't the last time Amy helped me navigate unfamiliar terrain. Law school is a three-year obstacle course of life and career decisions. One the one hand, it's nice to have so many opportunities. On the other hand, I had no idea what to do with those opportunities or any clue which opportunities served some long-term goal. Hell, I didn't even have a long-term goal. I just wanted to graduate and get a good job. I had some vague notion that I'd like to do public service after I repaid my law school debt. But I didn't have a job in mind.

Life didn't wait. Almost immediately after I committed to a law firm, people started talking about clerkship applications for after graduation. Judicial clerkships are one-year stints with federal judges. It's a fantastic learning experience for young lawyers: Clerks read court filings, research legal issues for a judge, and even help the judge draft opinions. Every former clerk raves about the experience, and private-sector employers often shell out tens of thousands in signing bonuses for recent clerks.

That's what I knew about clerkships, and it was completely true. It was also very superficial: The clerkship process is infinitely more complex. First you have to decide what kind of court you want to work for: a court that does a lot of trials or a court that hears appeals from lower courts. Then you have to decide which regions of the country to apply to. If you want to clerk for the Supreme Court, certain "feeder" judges give you a greater chance of doing so. Predictably, those judges hire more competitively, so holding out for a feeder judge carries certain risks—if you win the game, you're halfway to the chambers of the nation's highest court; if you lose, you're stuck without a clerkship. Sprinkled on top of these factors is the reality that you work closely with these judges. And no one wants to waste a year getting berated by an asshole in black robes.

There's no database that spits out this information, no central source that tells you which judges are nice, which judges send people to the Supreme Court, and which type of work—trial or appellate—you want to do. In fact, it's considered almost unseemly to talk about these things. How do you ask a professor if the judge he's recommending you to is a nice lady? It's trickier than it might seem.

So to get this information, you have to tap into your social network—student groups, friends who have clerked, and the few professors who are willing to give brutally honest advice. By this point in my law school experience, I had learned that the only way to take advantage of networking was to ask. So I did. Amy Chua told me that I shouldn't worry about clerking for a prestigious feeder judge because the credential wouldn't prove very useful, given my ambitions. But I pushed until she relented and agreed to recommend me to a high-powered federal judge with deep connections to multiple Supreme Court justices.

I submitted all the materials—a résumé, a polished writing sample, and a desperate letter of interest. I didn't know why I was doing it. Maybe, with my Southern drawl and lack of a family pedigree, I felt like I needed proof that I belonged at Yale Law. Or maybe I was just following the herd. Regardless of the reason, I *needed* to have this credential.

A few days after I submitted my materials, Amy called me into her office to let me know that I had made the short list. My heart fluttered. I knew that all I needed was an interview and I'd get the job. And I knew that if she pushed my application hard enough, I'd get the interview.

That was when I learned the value of real social capital. I don't mean to suggest that my professor picked up the phone and told the judge he had to give me an interview. Before she did that, my professor told me that she wanted to talk to me very seriously. She turned downright somber: "I don't think you're doing this for the right reasons. I think you're doing this for the credential, which is fine, but the credential doesn't actually serve your career goals. If you don't want to be a high-powered Supreme Court litigator, you shouldn't care that much about this job."

She then told me how hard a clerkship with this judge would be. He was demanding to the extreme. His clerks didn't take a single day off for an entire year. Then she got personal. She knew I had a new girlfriend and that I was crazy about her. "This clerkship is the type of thing that destroys relationships. If you want my advice, I think you should prioritize Usha and figure out a career move that actually suits you."

It was the best advice anyone has ever given me, and I took it. I told her to withdraw my application. It's impossible to say whether I would have gotten the job. I was probably being over-confident: My grades and résumé were fine but not fantastic. However, Amy's advice stopped me from making a life-altering decision. It prevented me from moving a thousand miles away from the person I eventually married. Most important, it allowed me to accept my place at this unfamiliar institution—it was okay to chart my own path and okay to put a girl above some short-sighted ambition. My professor gave me permission to be me.

It's hard to put a dollar value on that advice. It's the kind of thing that continues to pay dividends. But make no mistake: The advice had tangible economic value. Social capital isn't manifest only in someone connecting you to a friend or passing a résumé on to an old boss. It is also, or perhaps primarily, a measure of how much we learn through our friends, colleagues, and mentors. I didn't know how to prioritize my options, and I didn't know that there were other, better paths for me. I learned those things through my network—specifically, a very generous professor.

My education in social capital continues. For a time, I contributed to the website of David Frum, the journalist and opinion leader who now writes for *The Atlantic*. When I was ready to commit to one D.C. law firm, he suggested another firm where two of his friends from the Bush administration had recently taken senior partnerships. One of those friends interviewed me and, when I joined his firm, became an important mentor. I later ran into this man at a Yale conference, where he introduced me to his old buddy from the Bush White House (and my political hero), Indiana governor Mitch Daniels. Without David's advice, I never would have found myself at that firm, nor would I have spoken (albeit briefly) to the public figure I most admired.

I did decide that I wanted to clerk. But instead of walking into the process blindly, I came to know what I wanted out of the experience—to work for someone I respected, to learn as much as I could, and to be close to Usha. So Usha and I decided to go through the clerkship process together. We landed in northern Kentucky, not far from where I grew up. It was the best possible situation. We liked our judicial bosses so much that we asked them to officiate our wedding.

This is just one version of how the world of successful people actually works. But social capital is all around us. Those who tap into it and use it prosper. Those who don't are running life's race with a major handicap. This is a serious problem for kids like me. Here's a non-exhaustive list of things I didn't know when I got to Yale Law School:

That you needed to wear a suit to a job interview.

That wearing a suit large enough to fit a silverback gorilla was inappropriate.

That a butter knife wasn't just decorative (after all, anything that requires a butter knife can be done better with a spoon or an index finger).

That pleather and leather were different substances.

That your shoes and belt should match.

That certain cities and states had better job prospects.

That going to a nicer college brought benefits outside of bragging rights.

That finance was an industry that people worked in.

Mamaw always resented the hillbilly stereotype—the idea that our people were a bunch of slobbering morons. But the fact is that I was remarkably ignorant of how to get ahead. Not knowing things that many others do often has serious economic consequences. It cost me a job in college (apparently Marine Corps combat boots and khaki pants aren't proper interview attire) and could have cost me a lot more in law school if I hadn't had a few people helping me every step of the way.

Chapter 14

As I started my second year of law school, I felt like I'd made it. Fresh off a summer job at the U.S. Senate, I returned to New Haven with a wealth of new friends and experiences. I had this beautiful girlfriend, and I had a great job at a nice law firm almost in hand. I knew that kids like me weren't supposed to get this far, and I congratulated myself for having beaten the odds. I was better than where I came from: better than Mom and her addiction and better than the father figures who'd walked out on me. I regretted only that Mamaw and Papaw weren't around to see it.

But there were signs that things weren't going so well, particularly in my relationship with Usha. We'd been dating for only a few months when she stumbled upon an analogy that described me perfectly. I was, she said, a turtle. "Whenever something bad happens—even a hint of disagreement—you withdraw completely. It's like you have a shell that you hide in."

It was true. I had no idea how to deal with relationship problems, so I chose not to deal with them at all. I could scream at her when she did something I didn't like, but that seemed mean. Or I could withdraw and get away. Those were the proverbial arrows in my quiver, and I had nothing else. The thought of fighting with her reduced me to a morass of the qualities I thought I hadn't inherited from my family: stress, sadness, fear, anxiety. It was all there, and it was *intense*.

So I tried to get away, but Usha wouldn't let me. I tried to break everything off multiple times, but she told me that was stupid unless I didn't care about her. So I'd scream and I'd yell. I'd do all of the hateful things that my mother had done. And then I'd feel guilty and desperately afraid. For so much of my life, I'd made Mom out to be a kind of villain. And now I was acting like her. Nothing compares to the fear that you're becoming the monster in your closet.

During that second year of law school, Usha and I traveled to D.C. for follow-up interviews with a few law firms. I returned to our hotel room, dejected that I had just performed poorly with one of the firms I really wanted to work for. When Usha tried to comfort me, to tell me that I'd probably done better than I expected, but that even if I hadn't, there were other fish in the sea, I exploded. "Don't tell me that I did fine," I yelled. "You're just making an excuse for weakness. I didn't get here by making excuses for failure."

I stormed out of the room and spent the next couple of hours on the streets of D.C.'s business district. I thought about that time Mom took me and our toy poodle to Middletown's Comfort Inn after a screaming match with Bob. We stayed there for a couple of days, until Mamaw convinced Mom that she had to return home and face her problems like an adult. And I thought about Mom during her childhood, running out the back door with her mother and sister to avoid another night of terror with her alcoholic father. I was a third-generation escaper.

I was near Ford's Theatre, the historic location where John Wilkes Booth shot Abraham Lincoln. About half a block from the theater is a corner store that sells Lincoln memorabilia. In it, a large Lincoln blow-up doll with an extraordinarily large grin gazes at those walking by. I felt like this inflatable Lincoln was mocking me. *Why the hell is he smiling?* I thought. Lincoln was melancholy to begin with, and if any place invoked a smile, surely it wouldn't be a stone's throw away from the place where someone shot him in the head.

I turned the corner, and after a few steps I saw Usha sitting on the steps of Ford's Theatre. She had run after me, worried about me being alone. I realized then that I had a problem—that I must confront whatever it was that had, for generations, caused those in my family to hurt those whom they loved. I apologized profusely to Usha. I expected her to tell me to go fuck myself, that it would take days to make up for what I'd done, that I was a terrible person. A sincere apology is a surrender, and when someone surrenders, you go in for the kill. But Usha wasn't interested in that. She calmly told me through her tears that it was never acceptable to run away, that she was worried, and that I had to learn how to talk to her. And then she gave me a hug and told me that she accepted my apology and was glad I was okay. That was the end of it.

Usha hadn't learned how to fight in the hillbilly school of hard knocks. The first time I visited her family for Thanksgiving, I was amazed at the lack of drama. Usha's mother didn't complain about her father behind his back. There were no suggestions that good family friends were liars or backstabbers, no angry exchanges between a man's wife and the same man's sister. Usha's parents seemed to genuinely like her grandmother and spoke of their siblings with love. When I asked her father about a relatively estranged family member, I expected to hear a rant about character flaws. What I heard instead was sympathy and a little sadness but primarily a life lesson: "I still call him regularly and check up on him. You can't just cast aside family members because they seem uninterested in you. You've got to make the effort, because they're family."

I tried to go to a counselor, but it was just too weird. Talking to some stranger about my feelings made me want to vomit. I did go to the library, and I learned that behavior I considered commonplace was the subject of pretty intense academic study. Psychologists call the everyday occurrences of my and Lindsay's life "adverse childhood experiences," or ACEs. ACEs are traumatic childhood events, and their consequences reach far into adulthood. The trauma need not be physical. The following events or feelings are some of the most common ACEs:

- being sworn at, insulted, or humiliated by parents
- being pushed, grabbed, or having something thrown at you
- feeling that your family didn't support each other
- having parents who were separated or divorced
- living with an alcoholic or a drug user
- living with someone who was depressed or attempted suicide
- watching a loved one be physically abused.

ACEs happen everywhere, in every community. But studies have shown that ACEs are far more common in my corner of the demographic world. A report by the Wisconsin Children's

Trust Fund showed that among those with a college degree or more (the non–working class), fewer than half had experienced an ACE. Among the working class, well over half had at least one ACE, while about 40 percent had multiple ACEs. This is really striking—four in every ten working-class people had faced multiple instances of childhood trauma. For the non–working class, that number was 29 percent.

I gave a quiz to Aunt Wee, Uncle Dan, Lindsay, and Usha that psychologists use to measure the number of ACEs a person has faced. Aunt Wee scored a seven—higher even than Lindsay and me, who each scored a six. Dan and Usha—the two people whose families seemed nice to the point of oddity—each scored a zero. The weird people were the ones who hadn't faced any childhood trauma.

Children with multiple ACEs are more likely to struggle with anxiety and depression, to suffer from heart disease and obesity, and to contract certain types of cancers. They're also more likely to underperform in school and suffer from relationship instability as adults. Even excessive shouting can damage a kid's sense of security and contribute to mental health and behavioral issues down the road.

Harvard pediatricians have studied the effect that childhood trauma has on the mind. In addition to later negative health consequences, the doctors found that constant stress can actually change the chemistry of a child's brain. Stress, after all, is triggered by a physiological reaction. It's the consequence of adrenaline and other hormones flooding our system, usually in response to some kind of stimulus. This is the classic fight-or-flight response that we learn about in grade school. It sometimes produces incredible feats of strength and bravery from ordinary people. It's how mothers can lift heavy objects when their children are trapped underneath, and how an unarmed elderly woman can fight off a mountain lion with her bare hands to save her husband.

Unfortunately, the fight-or-flight response is a destructive constant companion. As Dr. Nadine Burke Harris put it, the response is great "if you're in a forest and there's a bear. The problem is when that bear comes home from the bar every night." When that happens, the Harvard researchers found, the sector of the brain that deals with highly stressful situations takes over. "Significant stress in early childhood," they write, " . . . result[s] in a hyperresponsive or chronically activated physiologic stress response, along with increased potential for fear and anxiety." For kids like me, the part of the brain that deals with stress and conflict is always activated—the switch flipped indefinitely. We are constantly ready to fight or flee, because there is constant exposure to the bear, whether that bear is an alcoholic dad or an unhinged mom. We become hard-wired for conflict. And that wiring remains, even when there's no more conflict to be had.

It's not just fighting. By almost any measure, American working-class families experience a level of instability unseen elsewhere in the world. Consider, for instance, Mom's revolving door of father figures. No other country experiences anything like this. In France, the percentage of children exposed to three or more maternal partners is 0.5 percent—about one in two hundred. The second highest share is 2.6 percent, in Sweden, or about one in forty. In the United States, the figure is a shocking 8.2 percent—about one in twelve—and the figure is even higher in the working class. The most depressing part is that relationship instability, like home chaos, is a vicious cycle. As sociologists Paula Fornby and Andrew Cherlin found, a "growing body of literature suggests that children who experience multiple transitions in family structure may fare worse developmentally than children raised in stable two-parent families and perhaps even than children raised in stable, single-parent families."

For many kids, the first impulse is escape, but people who lurch toward the exit rarely choose the right door. This is how my aunt found herself married at sixteen to an abusive husband. It's how my mom, the salutatorian of her high school class, had both a baby and a divorce, but not a single college credit under her belt before her teenage years were over. Out of the frying pan and into the fire. Chaos begets chaos. Instability begets instability. Welcome to family life for the American hillbilly.

For me, understanding my past and knowing that I wasn't doomed gave me the hope and fortitude to deal with the demons of my youth. And though it's cliché, the best medicine was talking about it with the people who understood. I asked Aunt Wee if she had similar relationship experiences, and she answered almost reflexively: "Of course. I was always ready for battle with Dan," she told me. "Sometimes I'd even brace myself for a big argument—like physically put myself in a fighting position—before he stopped speaking." I was shocked. Aunt Wee and Dan have the most successful marriage I've seen. Even after twenty years, they interact like they started dating last year. Her marriage got even better, she said, only after she realized that she didn't have to be on guard all the time.

Lindsay told me the same. "When I fought with Kevin, I'd insult him and tell him to do what I knew he wanted to do anyway—leave. He'd always ask me, 'What's wrong with you? Why do you fight with me like I'm your enemy?'" The answer is that, in our home, it was often difficult to tell friend from foe. Sixteen years later, though, and Lindsay is still married.

I thought a lot about myself, about the emotional triggers I'd learned over eighteen years of living at home. I realized that I mistrusted apologies, as they were often used to convince you to lower your guard. It was an "I'm sorry" that convinced me to take that fateful car ride with Mom more than a decade earlier. And I began to understand why I used words as weapons: That's what everyone around me did; I did it to survive. Disagreements were war, and you played to win the game.

I didn't unlearn these lessons overnight. I continue to struggle with conflict, to fight the statistical odds that sometimes seem to bear down on me. Sometimes it's easier knowing that the statistics suggest I should be in jail or fathering my fourth illegitimate child. And sometimes it's harder—conflict and family breakdown seem like the destiny I can't possibly escape. In my worst moments, I convince myself that there is no exit, and no matter how much I fight old demons, they are as much an inheritance as my blue eyes and brown hair. The sad fact is that I couldn't do it without Usha. Even at my best, I'm a delayed explosion—I can be defused, but only with skill and precision. It's not just that I've learned to control myself but that Usha has learned how to manage me. Put two of me in the same home and you have a positively radioactive situation. It's no surprise that every single person in my family who has built a successful home—Aunt Wee, Lindsay, my cousin Gail—married someone from outside our little culture.

This realization shattered the narrative I told about my life. In my own head, I was better than my past. I was strong. I left town as soon as I could, served my country in the Marines, excelled at Ohio State, and made it to the country's top law school.

I had no demons, no character flaws, no problems. But that just wasn't true. The things I wanted most in the entire world—a happy partner and a happy home—required constant mental focus. My self-image was bitterness masquerading as arrogance. A few weeks into my second year of law school, I hadn't spoken to Mom in many months, longer than at any point in my life. I realized that of all the emotions I felt toward my mother— love, pity, forgiveness, anger, hatred, and dozens of others—I had never tried sympathy. I had never tried to understand my mom. At my most empathetic, I figured she suffered from some terrible genetic defect, and I hoped I hadn't inherited it. As I increasingly saw Mom's behavior in myself, I tried to understand her.

Uncle Jimmy told me that, long ago, he'd walked in on a discussion between Mamaw and Papaw. Mom had gotten herself in some trouble and they needed to bail her out. These bailouts were common, and they always came with theoretical strings attached. She had to budget, they'd tell her, and they'd put her on some arbitrary plan they'd designed themselves. The plan was the cost of their help. As they sat and discussed things, Papaw buried his head in his hands and did something Uncle Jimmy had never seen him do: He wept. "I've failed her," he cried. He kept on repeating, "I've failed her; I've failed her; I've failed my baby girl."

Papaw's rare breakdown strikes at the heart of an important question for hillbillies like me: How much of our lives, good and bad, should we credit to our personal decisions, and how much is just the inheritance of our culture, our families, and our parents who have failed their children? How much is Mom's life her own fault? Where does blame stop and sympathy begin?

All of us have opinions. Uncle Jimmy reacts viscerally to the idea that any of the blame for Mom's choices can be laid at Papaw's feet. "He didn't fail her. Whatever happened to her, it's her own damned fault." Aunt Wee sees things in much the same way, and who can blame her? Just nineteen months younger than Mom, she saw the worst of Mamaw and Papaw and made her own share of mistakes before coming out on the other side. If she can do it, then so should Mom. Lindsay has a bit more sympathy and thinks that just as our lives left us with demons, Mom's life must have done the same to her. But at some point, Lindsay says, you have to stop making excuses and take responsibility.

My own view is mixed. Whatever might be said about my mom's parents' roles in my life, their constant fighting and alcoholism must have taken its toll on her. Even when they were children, the fighting seemed to affect my aunt and mother differently. While Aunt Wee would plead with her parents to calm down, or provoke her father in order to take the heat off her mother, Mom would hide, or run away, or collapse on the floor with her hands over her ears. She didn't handle it as well as her brother and sister. In some ways, Mom is the Vance child who lost the game of statistics. If anything, my family is probably lucky that only one of them lost that game.

What I do know is that Mom is no villain. She loves Lindsay and me. She tried desperately to be a good mother. Sometimes she succeeded; sometimes she didn't. She tried to find happiness in love and work, but she listened too much to the wrong voice in her head. But Mom deserves much of the blame. No person's childhood gives him or her a perpetual moral get-out-of-jail-free card—not Lindsay, not Aunt Wee, not me, and not Mom.

Throughout my life, no one could inspire such intense emotions as my mom, not even Mamaw. When I was a kid, I loved her so much that when a kindergarten classmate made fun of her umbrella, I punched him in the face. When I watched her succumb again and again to addiction, I hated her and wished sometimes that she would take enough narcotics to rid me and Lindsay of her for good. When she lay sobbing in bed after another failed relationship, I felt a rage that could have driven me to kill.

Toward the end of law school, Lindsay called to tell me that Mom had taken to a new drug—heroin—and had decided to give rehab another try. I didn't know how many times Mom had been to rehab, how many nights she'd spent in the hospital barely conscious because of some drug. So I shouldn't have been surprised or all that bothered, but "heroin" just has a certain ring to it; it's like the Kentucky Derby of drugs. When I learned of Mom's newest substance of choice, I felt a cloud hanging over me for weeks. Maybe I had finally lost all hope for her.

The emotion Mom inspired then was not hatred, or love, or rage, but fear. Fear for her safety. Fear for Lindsay having to deal yet again with Mom's problems while I lived hundreds of miles away. Fear most of all that I hadn't escaped a goddamned thing. Months away from graduating from Yale Law, I should have felt on top of the world. Instead, I found myself wondering the same thing I'd wondered for much of the past year: whether people like us can ever truly change.

When Usha and I graduated, the crew that watched me walk across the stage numbered eighteen, including my cousins Denise and Gail, the daughters, respectively, of Mamaw's brothers David and Pet. Usha's parents and uncle—fantastic people, though considerably less rowdy than our crew—made the trip, too. It was the first time that her family met mine, and we behaved. (Though Denise had some choice words for the modern "art" at the museum we visited!)

Mom's bout with addiction ended as they always did—in an uneasy truce. She didn't make the trip to see me graduate, but she wasn't using drugs at that moment, and that was all right with me. Justice Sonya Sotomayor spoke at our commencement and advised that it was okay to be unsure about what we wanted to do with ourselves. I think she was talking about our careers, but for me it had a much broader meaning. I had learned much about law at Yale. But I'd also learned that this new world would always seem a bit foreign to me, and that being a hillbilly meant sometimes not knowing the difference between love and war. When we graduated, that's what I was most unsure about.

Chapter 15

What I remember most is the fucking spiders. Really big ones, like tarantulas or something. I stood at a window of one of those sleazy roadside motels, separated from a woman (who certainly hadn't majored in hospitality management) by a thick pane of glass. The light from her office illuminated a few spiderwebs suspended between the building and the makeshift sun blocker that seemed primed to collapse on top of me. On each web was at least one giant spider, and I thought that if I looked away from them for too long, one of those ghastly creatures would jump on my face and suck my blood. I'm not even afraid of spiders, but these things were *big*.

I wasn't supposed to be here. I'd structured my entire life to avoid just these types of places. When I thought of leaving my hometown, of "getting out," it was from this sort of place that I wanted to escape. It was past midnight. The streetlight revealed the silhouette of a man sitting halfway in his truck—the door open, his feet dangling to the side—with the unmistakable form of a hypodermic needle sticking from his arm. I should have been shocked, but this was Middletown, after all. Just a few weeks earlier, the police had discovered a woman passed out at the local car wash, a bag of heroin and a spoon in the passenger seat, the needle still protruding from her arm.

The woman running the hotel that night was the most pitiful sight of all. She might have been forty, but everything about her—from the long, gray, greasy hair, the mouth empty of teeth, and the frown that she wore like a millstone—screamed old age. This woman had lived a hard life. Her voice sounded like a small child's, even a toddler's. It was meek, barely audible, and very sad.

I gave the woman my credit card, and she was clearly unprepared. "Normally, people pay cash," she explained. I told her, "Yeah, but like I said on the phone, I'm going to pay with a credit card. I can run to an ATM if you'd prefer." "Oh, I'm sorry, I guess I forgot. But it's okay, we've got one of those machines around here somewhere." So she retrieved one of those ancient card-swiping machines—the kind that imprints the card's information on a yellow slip of paper. When I handed her the card, her eyes seemed to plead with me, as if she were a prisoner in her own life. "Enjoy your stay," she said, which struck me as an odd instruction. I had told her on the phone not an hour earlier that the room wasn't for me, it was for my homeless mother. "Okay," I said. "Thanks."

I was a recent graduate of Yale Law School, a former editor of the prestigious *Yale Law Journal*, and a member of the bar in good standing. Just two months earlier, Usha and I were married on a beautiful day in Eastern Kentucky. My entire family showed up for the occasion, and we both changed our name to Vance—giving me, finally, the same name as the family to which I belonged. I had a nice job, a recently purchased home, a loving relationship, and a happy life in a city I loved—Cincinnati. Usha and I had returned there for a year after law school for one-year clerkships and had built a home with our two dogs. I was upwardly mobile. I had made it. I had achieved the American Dream.

Or at least that's how it looked to an outsider. But upward mobility is never clean-cut, and the world I left always finds a way to reel me back in. I don't know the precise chain of events that led me to that hotel, but I knew the stuff that mattered. Mom had begun using again. She'd stolen some family heirlooms from her fifth husband to buy drugs (prescription opiates, I think), and he'd kicked her out of the house in response. They were divorcing, and she had nowhere to go.

I'd sworn to myself that I'd never help Mom again, but the person who made that oath to himself had changed. I was exploring, however uneasily, the Christian faith that I'd discarded years earlier. I had learned, for the first time, the extent of Mom's childhood emotional wounds. And I had realized that those wounds never truly heal, even for me. So when I discovered that Mom was in dire straits, I didn't mutter insults under my breath and hang up the phone. I offered to help her.

I tried to call a Middletown hotel and give them my credit card information. The cost for a week was a hundred and fifty dollars, and I figured that would give us time to come up with a plan. But they wouldn't accept my card over the phone, so at eleven P.M. on a Tuesday night, I drove from Cincinnati to Middletown (about an hour's drive each way) to keep Mom from homelessness.

The plan I developed seemed relatively simple. I'd give Mom enough money to help her get on her feet. She'd find her own place, save money to get her nursing license back, and go from there. In the meantime, I'd monitor her finances to ensure that she stayed clean and on track financially. It reminded me of the "plans" Mamaw and Papaw used to put together, but I convinced myself that this time things would be different.

I'd like to say that helping Mom came easily. That I had made some peace with my past and was able to fix a problem that had plagued me since elementary school. That, armed with sympathy and an understanding of Mom's childhood, I was able to patiently help Mom deal with her addiction. But dealing with that sleazy motel was hard. And actively managing her finances, as I planned to do, required more patience and time than I had.

By the grace of God, I no longer hide from Mom. But I can't fix everything, either. There is room now for both anger at Mom for the life she chooses and sympathy for the childhood she didn't. There is room to help when I can, when finances and emotional reserves allow me to care in the way Mom needs. But there is also recognition of my own limitations and my willingness to separate myself from Mom when engagement means too little money to pay my own bills or too little patience left over for the people who matter most. That's the uneasy truce I've struck with myself, and it works for now.

People sometimes ask whether I think there's anything we can do to "solve" the problems of my community. I know what they're looking for: a magical public policy solution or an innovative government program. But these problems of family, faith, and culture aren't like a Rubik's Cube, and I don't think that solutions (as most understand the term) really exist. A good friend, who worked for a time in the White House and cares deeply about the plight of the working class, once told me, "The best way to look at this might be to recognize that you probably can't fix these things. They'll always be around. But maybe you can put your thumb on the scale a little for the people at the margins."

There were many thumbs put on my scale. When I look back
at my life, what jumps out is how many variables had to fall in
place in order to give me a chance. There was my grandparents'
constant presence, even when my mother and stepfather moved
far away in an effort to shut them out. Despite the revolving
door of would-be father figures, I was often surrounded by caring
and kind men. Even with her faults, Mom instilled in me a lifelong love of education and learning. My sister always protected
me, even after I'd physically outgrown her. Dan and Aunt Wee
opened their home when I was too afraid to ask. Long before
that, they were my first real exemplars of a happy and loving
marriage. There were teachers, distant relatives, and friends.

Remove any of these people from the equation, and I'm probably screwed. Other people who have overcome the odds cite the
same sorts of interventions. Jane Rex runs the transfer students'
office at Appalachian State University. Like me, she grew up in
a working-class family and was its first member to attend college. She's also been married for nearly forty years and has raised
three successful kids of her own. Ask what made a difference in
her life, and she'll tell you about the stable family that empowered her and gave her a sense of control over her future. And
she'll tell you about the power of seeing enough of the world to
dream big: "I think you have to have good role models around
you. One of my very good friends, her father was the president
of the bank, so I got to see different things. I knew there was
another life out there, and that exposure gives you something
to dream for."

My cousin Gail is one of my all-time favorite people: She's one
of the first of my mom's generation, the Blanton grandchildren.
Gail's life is the American Dream personified: a beautiful house,

three great kids, a happy marriage, and a saintly demeanor. Outside of Mamaw Blanton, a virtual deity in the eyes of us grandkids and great-grandkids, I've never heard anyone else called "the nicest person in the world." For Gail, it's an entirely deserved title.

I assumed that Gail had inherited her storybook life from her parents. *No one's that nice,* I thought, especially not someone who's suffered any real adversity. But Gail was a Blanton, and, at heart a hillbilly, and I should have known that no hillbilly makes it to adulthood without a few major screwups along the way. Gail's home life provided its own emotional baggage. She was seven when her dad walked out and seventeen when she graduated from high school, planning for college at Miami University. But there was a catch: "Mom told me I couldn't go to college unless I broke up with my boyfriend. So I moved out the day after graduation, and by August, I was pregnant."

Almost immediately, her life began to disintegrate. Racial prejudice bubbled to the surface when she announced that a black baby was joining the family. Announcements led to arguments, and then one day Gail found herself without a family. "I didn't hear from any of our relatives," Gail told me. "My mom said she never wanted to hear my name again."

Given her age and the lack of family support, it's hardly surprising that her marriage soon ended. But Gail's life had grown considerably more complex: She hadn't just lost her family, she'd gained a young daughter who depended entirely on her. "It completely changed my life—being a mom was my identity. I might have been a hippie, but now I had rules—no drugs, no alcohol, nothing that was going to lead to social services taking my baby away."

So here's Gail: teenage single mom, no family, little support. A lot of people would wilt in those circumstances, but the hillbilly took over. "Dad wasn't really around," Gail remembered, "and hadn't been in years, and I obviously wasn't speaking to Mom. But I remember the one lesson I took from them, and that was that we could do anything we wanted. I wanted that baby, and I wanted to make it work. So I did it." She got a job with a local telephone company, worked her way up the ladder, and even returned to college. By the time she remarried, she had hit one hell of a stride. The storybook marriage to her second husband, Allan, is just icing on the cake.

Some version of Gail's story often rears its head where I grew up. You watch as teenagers find themselves in dire straits, sometimes of their own making and sometimes not. The statistics are stacked high against them, and many succumb: to crime or an early death at worst, domestic strife and welfare dependency at best. But others make it. There's Jane Rex. There's Lindsay, who blossomed in the midst of Mamaw's death; Aunt Wee, who put her life on track after ditching an abusive husband. Each benefited from the same types of experiences in one way or another. They had a family member they could count on. And they saw— from a family friend, an uncle, or a work mentor—what was available and what was possible.

Not long after I began thinking about what might help the American working class get ahead, a team of economists, including Raj Chetty, published a groundbreaking study on opportunity in America. Unsurprisingly, they found that a poor kid's chances of rising through the ranks of America's meritocracy were lower than most of us wanted. By their metrics, a lot of European countries seemed better than America at the American

Dream. More important, they discovered that opportunity was not spread evenly over the whole country. In places like Utah, Oklahoma, and Massachusetts, the American Dream was doing just fine—as good or better than any other place in the world. It was in the South, the Rust Belt, and Appalachia where poor kids really struggled. Their findings surprised a lot of people, but not me. And not anyone who'd spent any time in these areas.

In a paper analyzing the data, Chetty and his coauthors noted two important factors that explained the uneven geographic distribution of opportunity: the prevalence of single parents and income segregation. Growing up around a lot of single moms and dads and living in a place where most of your neighbors are poor really narrows the realm of possibilities. It means that unless you have a Mamaw and Papaw to make sure you stay the course, you might never make it out. It means that you don't have people to show you by example what happens when you work hard and get an education. It means, essentially, that everything that made it possible for me, Lindsay, Gail, Jane Rex, and Aunt Wee to find some measure of happiness is missing. So I wasn't surprised that Mormon Utah—with its strong church, integrated communities, and intact families—wiped the floor with Rust Belt Ohio.

There are, I think, policy lessons to draw from my life—ways we might put our thumb on that all-important scale. We can adjust how our social services systems treat families like mine. Remember that when I was twelve I watched Mom get hauled away in a police cruiser. I'd seen her get arrested before, but I knew that this time was different. We were in the system now, with social worker visits and mandated family counseling. And a court date hanging over my head like a guillotine blade.

Ostensibly, the caseworkers were there to protect me, but it became very obvious, very early in the process, that they were obstacles to overcome. When I explained that I spent most of my time with my grandparents and that I'd like to continue with that arrangement, they replied that the courts would not necessarily sanction such an arrangement. In the eyes of the law, my grandmother was an untrained caretaker without a foster license. If things went poorly for my mother in the courts, I was as likely to find myself with a foster family as I was with Mamaw. The notion of being separated from everyone and everything I loved was terrifying. So I shut my mouth, told the social workers everything was fine, and hoped that I wouldn't lose my family when the court hearing came.

That hope panned out—Mom didn't go to jail, and I got to stay with Mamaw. The arrangement was informal: I could stay with Mom if I wanted, but if not, Mamaw's door was always open. The enforcement mechanism was equally informal: Mamaw would kill anyone who tried to keep me from her. This worked for us because Mamaw was a lunatic and our entire family feared her.

Not everyone can rely on the saving graces of a crazy hillbilly. Child services are, for many kids, the last pieces of the safety net; if they fall through, precious little remains to catch them.

Part of the problem is how state laws define the family. For families like mine—and for many black and Hispanic families—grandparents, cousins, aunts, and uncles play an outsize role. Child services often cut them out of the picture, as they did in my case. Some states require occupational licensing for foster parents—just like nurses and doctors—even when the would-be foster parent is a grandmother or another close family member. In other words, our country's social services weren't made for hillbilly families, and they often make a bad problem worse.

I wish I could say this was a small problem, but it's not. In a given year, 640,000 children, most of them poor, will spend at least some time in foster care. Add that to the unknown number of kids who face abuse or neglect but somehow avoid the foster care system, and you have an epidemic—one that current policies exacerbate.

There are other things we can do. We can build policies based on a better understanding of what stands in the way of kids like me. The most important lesson of my life is not that society failed to provide me with opportunities. My elementary and middle schools were entirely adequate, staffed with teachers who did everything they could to reach me. Our high school ranked near the bottom of Ohio's schools, but that had little to do with the staff and much to do with the students. I had Pell Grants and government-subsidized low-interest student loans that made college affordable, and need-based scholarships for law school. I never went hungry, thanks at least in part to the old-age benefits that Mamaw generously shared with me. These programs are far from perfect, but to the degree that I nearly succumbed to my worst decisions (and I came quite close), the fault lies almost entirely with factors outside the government's control.

Recently, I sat down with a group of teachers from my alma mater, Middletown High. All of them expressed the worry, in one form or another, that society devoted too many resources too late in the game. "It's like our politicians think college is the only way," one teacher told me. "For many, it's great. But a lot of our kids have no realistic shot of getting a college degree." Another said: "The violence and the fighting, it's all they've seen from a very young age. One of my students lost her baby like she'd lost her car keys—had no idea where it went. Two weeks later, her child turned up in New York City with the father, a drug dealer, and some of his family." Short of a miracle, we all know what kind of life awaits that poor baby. Yet there's precious little to support her now, when an intervention might help.

So I think that any successful policy program would recognize what my old high school's teachers see every day: that the real problem for so many of these kids is what happens (or doesn't happen) at home. For example, we'd recognize that Section 8 vouchers ought to be administered in a way that doesn't segregate the poor into little enclaves. As Brian Campbell, another Middletown teacher, told me, "When you have a large base of Section 8 parents and kids supported by fewer middle-class taxpayers, it's an upside-down triangle. There're fewer emotional and financial resources when the only people in a neighborhood are low-income. You just can't lump them together, because then you have a bigger pool of hopelessness." On the other hand, he said, "put the lower-income kids with those who have a different lifestyle model, and the lower-income kids start to rise up." Yet when Middletown recently tried to limit the number of Section 8 vouchers offered within certain neighborhoods, the federal government balked. Better, I suppose, to keep those kids cut off from the middle class.

Government policy may be powerless to resolve other problems in our community. As a child, I associated accomplishments in school with femininity. Manliness meant strength, courage, a willingness to fight, and, later, success with girls. Boys who got good grades were "sissies" or "faggots." I don't know where I got this feeling. Certainly not from Mamaw, who demanded good grades, nor from Papaw. But it was there, and studies now show that working-class boys like me do much worse in school because they view schoolwork as a feminine endeavor. Can you change this with a new law or program? Probably not. Some scales aren't that amenable to the proverbial thumb.

I've learned that the very traits that enabled my survival during childhood inhibit my success as an adult. I see conflict and I run away or prepare for battle. This makes little sense in my current relationships, but without that attitude, my childhood homes would have consumed me. I learned early to spread my money out lest Mom or someone else find it and "borrow" it—some under the mattress, some in the underwear drawer, some at Mamaw's house. When, later in life, Usha and I consolidated finances, she was shocked to learn that I had multiple bank accounts and small past-due balances on credit cards. Usha still sometimes reminds me that not every perceived slight—from a passing motorist or a neighbor critical of my dogs—is cause for a blood feud. And I always concede, despite my raw emotions, that she's probably right.

A couple of years ago, I was driving in Cincinnati with Usha, when somebody cut me off. I honked, the guy flipped me off, and when we stopped at a red light (with this guy in front of me), I unbuckled my seat belt and opened the car door. I planned to demand an apology (and fight the guy if necessary), but my common sense prevailed and I shut the door before I got out of the car. Usha was delighted that I'd changed my mind before she yelled at me to stop acting like a lunatic (which has happened in the past), and she told me that she was proud of me for resisting my natural instinct. The other driver's sin was to insult my honor, and it was on that honor that nearly every element of my happiness depended as a child—it kept the school bully from messing with me, connected me to my mother when some man or his children insulted her (even if I agreed with the substance of the insult), and gave me something, however small, over which I exercised complete control. For the first eighteen or so years of my life, standing down would have earned me a verbal lashing as a "pussy" or a "wimp" or a "girl." The objectively correct course of action was something that the majority of my life had taught me was repulsive to an upstanding young man. For a few hours after I did the right thing, I silently criticized myself. But that's progress, right? Better that than sitting in a jail cell for teaching that asshole a lesson about defensive driving.

Conclusion

Shortly before Christmas last year, I stood in the kids' section of a Washington, D.C., Walmart, shopping list in hand, gazing at toys and talking myself out of each of them. That year, I had volunteered to "adopt" a needy child, which meant that I was given a list by the local branch of the Salvation Army and told to return with a bag of unwrapped Christmas gifts.

It sounds pretty simple, but I managed to find fault with nearly every suggestion. Pajamas? Poor people don't wear pajamas. We fall asleep in our underwear or blue jeans. To this day, I find the very notion of pajamas an unnecessary elite indulgence, like caviar or electric ice cube makers. There was a toy guitar that I thought looked both fun and enriching, but I remembered the electronic keyboard my grandparents had given me one year and how one of Mom's boyfriends meanly ordered me to "shut that fucking thing up." I passed on learning aids for fear of appearing condescending. Eventually I settled on some clothes, a fake cell phone, and fire trucks.

I grew up in a world where everyone worried about how they'd pay for Christmas. Now I live in one where opportunities abound for the wealthy and privileged to shower their generosity on the community's poor. Many prestigious law firms sponsor an "angel program," which assigns a child to a lawyer and provides a wish list of gifts. Usha's former courthouse encouraged judicial employees to adopt a kid for the holidays—each a child of someone who previously went through the court system. Program coordinators hoped that if someone else purchased presents, the child's parents might feel less tempted to commit crimes in order to provide. And there's always Toys for Tots. During the past few Christmas seasons, I've found myself in large department stores, buying toys for kids I've never met.

As I shop, I'm reminded that wherever I fell on the American socioeconomic ladder as a child, others occupy much lower rungs: children who cannot depend on the generosity of grandparents for Christmas gifts; parents whose financial situations are so dire that they rely on criminal conduct—rather than payday loans—to put today's hot toys under the tree. This is a very useful exercise. As scarcity has given way to plenty in my own life, these moments of retail reflection force me to consider just how lucky I am.

Still, shopping for low-income kids reminds me of my childhood and of the ways that Christmas gifts can serve as domestic land mines. Every year the parents in my neighborhood would begin an annual ritual very different from the one I've become accustomed to in my new material comfort: worrying about how to give their kids a "nice Christmas," with niceness always defined by the bounty underneath the Christmas tree. If your friends came over the week before Christmas and saw a barren floor beneath the tree, you would offer a justification. "Mom just hasn't gone shopping yet" or "Dad's waiting for a big paycheck at the end of the year, and then he'll get a ton of stuff." These excuses were meant to mask what everyone knew: All of us were poor, and no amount of Teenage Mutant Ninja Turtles memorabilia would change that.

No matter our financial position, our family somehow managed to spend just more than we had on holiday shopping. We didn't qualify for credit cards, but there were many ways to spend money you didn't have. You could write a future date on a check (a practice called "post-dating") so the recipient couldn't cash it until you had money in the bank. You could draw a short-term loan from a payday lender. If all else failed, you could borrow money from the grandparents. Indeed, I recall many winter conversations in which Mom pleaded with Mamaw and Papaw to lend her money to ensure that their grandchildren had a nice Christmas. They'd always protest Mom's understanding of what made Christmas nice, but they'd still give in. It might be the day before Christmas, but our tree would be piled high with the trendiest gifts even as our family savings dwindled from very little to nothing, then from nothing to something less than that.

When I was a baby, Mom and Lindsay frantically searched for a Teddy Ruxpin doll, a toy so popular that every store in town sold out. It was expensive and, as I was only two, unnecessary. But Lindsay still remembers the day wasted searching for the toy. Mom somehow received a tip about a stranger who was willing to part with one of his Ruxpins at a significant markup. Mom and Lindsay traveled to his house to fetch the trinket that stood between a child who could barely walk and the Christmas of his dreams. The only thing I remember of old Teddy is finding him in a box years later, his sweater tattered and his face covered in crusted snot.

It was the holiday season that taught me about tax refunds, which I gathered were free bits of money sent to the poor in the new year to save them from the financial indiscretions of the old one. Income tax refunds were the ultimate backstops. "We can definitely afford this; we'll just pay for it with the refund check" became a Christmas mantra. But the government was fickle. There were few moments more anxious than the one when Mom came home from the tax preparer in early January. Sometimes the refund exceeded expectations. But when Mom learned that Uncle Sam couldn't cover the Christmas splurge because her "credits" weren't as high as she had hoped, that could ruin your whole month. Ohio Januaries are depressing enough as it is.

I assumed that rich people celebrated Christmas just like us, perhaps with fewer financial worries and even cooler presents. Yet I noticed after my cousin Bonnie was born that Christmastime at Aunt Wee's house had a decidedly different flavor. Somehow my aunt and uncle's children ended up with more pedestrian gifts than I had come to expect as a child. There was no obsession with meeting a two- or three-hundred-dollar threshold for each child, no worry that a kid would suffer in the absence of the newest electronic gadget. Usha often received books for Christmas. My cousin Bonnie, at the age of eleven, asked her parents to donate her Christmas gifts to Middletown's needy. Shockingly, her parents obliged: They didn't define their family's Christmas holiday by the dollar value of gifts their daughter accumulated.

However you want to define these two groups and their approach to giving—rich and poor; educated and uneducated; upper-class and working-class—their members increasingly occupy two separate worlds. As a cultural emigrant from one group to the other, I am acutely aware of their differences.

Sometimes I view members of the elite with an almost primal scorn—recently, an acquaintance used the word "confabulate" in a sentence, and I just wanted to scream. But I have to give it to them: Their children are happier and healthier, their divorce rates lower, their church attendance higher, their lives longer. These people are beating us at our own damned game.

I was able to escape the worst of my culture's inheritance. And uneasy though I am about my new life, I cannot whine about it: The life I lead now was the stuff of fantasy during my childhood. So many people helped create that fantasy. At every level of my life and in every environment, I have found family and mentors and lifelong friends who supported and enabled me.

But I often wonder: Where would I be without them? I think back on my freshman year of high school, a grade I nearly failed, and the morning when Mom walked into Mamaw's house demanding a cup of clean urine. Or years before that, when I was a lonely kid with two fathers, neither of whom I saw very often, and Papaw decided that he would be the best dad he could be for as long as he lived. Or the months I spent with Lindsay, a teenage girl acting as a mother while our own mother lived in a treatment center. Or the moment I can't even remember when Papaw installed a secret phone line in the bottom of my toy box so that Lindsay could call Mamaw and Papaw if things got a little too crazy. Thinking about it now, about how close I was to the abyss, gives me chills. I am one lucky son of a bitch.

Not long ago, I had lunch with Brian, a young man who reminded me of fifteen-year-old J.D. Like Mom, his mother caught a taste for narcotics, and like me, he has a complicated relationship with his father. He's a sweet kid with a big heart and a quiet manner. He has spent nearly his entire life in Appalachian Kentucky; we went to lunch at a local fast-food restaurant, because in that corner of the world there isn't much else to eat. As we talked, I noticed little quirks that few others would. He didn't want to share his milk shake, which was a little out of character for a kid who ended every sentence with "please" or "thank you." He finished his food quickly and then nervously looked from person to person. I could tell that he wanted to ask a question, so I wrapped my arm around his shoulder and asked if he needed anything. "Y—Yeah," he started, refusing to make eye contact. And then, almost in a whisper: "I wonder if I could get a few more french fries?" He was hungry. In 2014, in the richest country on earth, he wanted a little extra to eat but felt uncomfortable asking. Lord help us.

Just a few months after we saw each other last, Brian's mom died unexpectedly. He hadn't lived with her in years, so outsiders might imagine that her death was easier to bear. Those folks are wrong. People like Brian and me don't lose contact with our parents because we don't care; we lose contact with them to survive. We never stop loving, and we never lose hope that our loved ones will change. Rather, we are forced, either by wisdom or by the law, to take the path of self-preservation.

What happens to Brian? He has no Mamaw or Papaw, at least not like mine, and though he's lucky enough to have supportive family who will keep him out of foster care, his hope of a "normal life" evaporated long ago, if it ever existed. When we met, his mother had already permanently lost custody. In his short life, he has already experienced multiple instances of childhood trauma, and in a few years he will begin making decisions about employment and education that even children of wealth and privilege have trouble navigating.

Any chance he has lies with the people around him—his family, me, my kin, the people like us, and the broad community of hillbillies. And if that chance is to materialize, we hillbillies must wake the hell up. Brian's mom's death was another shitty card in an already abysmal hand, but there are many cards left to deal: whether his community empowers him with a sense that he can control his own destiny or encourages him to take refuge in resentment at forces beyond his control; whether he can access a church that teaches him lessons of Christian love, family, and purpose; whether those people who do step up to positively influence Brian find emotional and spiritual support from their neighbors.

I believe we hillbillies are the toughest goddamned people on this earth. We take an electric saw to the hide of those who insult our mother. We make young men consume cotton undergarments to protect a sister's honor. But are we tough enough to do what needs to be done to help a kid like Brian? Are we tough enough to build a church that forces kids like me to engage with the world rather than withdraw from it? Are we tough enough to look ourselves in the mirror and admit that our conduct harms our children?

Public policy can help, but there is no government that can fix these problems for us.

Recall how my cousin Mike sold his mother's house—a property that had been in our family for over a century—because he couldn't trust his own neighbors not to ransack it. Mamaw refused to purchase bicycles for her grandchildren because they kept disappearing—even when locked up—from her front porch. She feared answering her door toward the end of her life because an able-bodied woman who lived next door would not stop bothering her for cash—money, we later learned, for drugs. These problems were not created by governments or corporations or anyone else. We created them, and only we can fix them.

We don't need to live like the elites of California, New York, or Washington, D.C. We don't need to work a hundred hours a week at law firms and investment banks. We don't need to socialize at cocktail parties. We do need to create a space for the J.D.s and Brians of the world to have a chance. I don't know what the answer is, precisely, but I know it starts when we stop blaming Obama or Bush or faceless companies and ask ourselves what we can do to make things better.

I wanted to ask Brian whether, like me, he had bad dreams. For nearly two decades, I suffered from a terrible recurring nightmare. The first time it came to me, I was seven, fast asleep in my great Mamaw Blanton's bed. In the dream, I'm trapped in large conference room in a large tree house—as if the Keebler elves had just finished a massive picnic and their tree house were still adorned with dozens of tables and chairs. I'm there alone with Lindsay and Mamaw, when all of a sudden Mom charges through the room, tossing tables and chairs as she goes. She screams, but her voice is robotic and distorted, as if filtered through radio static. Mamaw and Lindsay run for a hole in the floor—presumably the exit ladder from the tree house. I fall behind, and by the time I reach the exit, Mom is just behind me. I wake up, right as she's about to grab me, when I realize not just that the monster has caught me but that Mamaw and Lindsay have abandoned me.

In different versions, the antagonist changes form. It has been a Marine Corps drill instructor, a barking dog, a movie villain, and a mean teacher. Mamaw and Lindsay always make an appearance, and they always make it to the exit just ahead of me.

Without fail, the dream provokes pure terror. The first time I had it, I woke up and ran to Mamaw, who was up late watching TV. I explained the dream and begged her never to leave me. She promised that she wouldn't and stroked my hair until I fell asleep again.

My subconscious had spared me for years, when, out of nowhere, I had the dream again a few weeks after I graduated from law school. There was a crucial difference: The subject of the monster's ire wasn't me but my dog, Casper, with whom I'd lost my temper earlier in the night. There was no Lindsay and no Mamaw. And I was the monster.

I chased my poor dog around the tree house, hoping to catch him and throttle him. But I felt Casper's terror, and I felt my shame at having lost my temper. I finally caught up to him, but I didn't wake up. Instead, Casper turned and looked at me with those sad, heart-piercing eyes that only dogs possess. So I didn't throttle him; I gave him a hug. And the last emotion I felt before waking was relief at having controlled my temper.

I got out of bed for a glass of cold water, and when I returned, Casper was staring at me, wondering what on earth his human was doing awake at such an odd hour. It was two o'clock in the morning—probably about the same time it was when I first woke from the terrifying dream over twenty years earlier. There was no Mamaw to comfort me. But there were my two dogs on the floor, and there was the love of my life lying in bed. Tomorrow I would go to work, take the dogs to the park, buy groceries with Usha, and make a nice dinner. It was everything I ever wanted. So I patted Casper's head and went back to sleep.

Acknowledgments

Writing this book was among the most challenging and rewarding experiences of my life. I learned much I didn't know about my culture, my neighborhood, and my family, and I relearned much that I had forgotten. I owe a great deal to many people. In no particular order:

Tina Bennett, my wonderful agent, believed in the project even before I did. She encouraged me when I needed it, pushed me when I needed it, and guided me through a publication process that initially scared the hell out of me. She has the heart of a hillbilly and the mind of a poet, and I'm honored to call her a friend.

Besides Tina, the person who deserves the most credit for this book's existence is Amy Chua, my Yale contracts professor, who convinced me that both my life and the conclusions I drew from it were worth putting down on paper. She has the wisdom of a respected academic and the confident delivery of a Tiger Mother, and there were many times that I needed (and benefitted) from both.

The entire team at Harper deserves tremendous credit. Jonathan Jao, my editor, helped me think critically about what I wanted the book to accomplish and had the patience to help me accomplish it. Sofia Groopman gave the book a fresh eye when it was desperately needed. Joanna, Tina, and Katie guided me through the publicity process with warmth and skill. Tim Duggan took a chance on this project and me when he had little reason to do so. For all of them, and their work on my behalf, I'm very thankful.

Many people read various drafts and offered important feedback, from questioning the choice of a word in a particular sentence to doubting the wisdom of deleting an entire chapter. Charles Tyler read a very early draft and forced me to hone in on a few core themes. Kyle Bumgarner and Sam Rudman offered helpful feedback early in the writing process. Kiel Brennan-Marquez, who has had the official and unofficial burden of teaching me writing for many years, read and critiqued multiple drafts. I appreciate all of their efforts.

I'm grateful to the many people who opened up about their lives and work, including Jane Rex, Sally Williamson, Jennifer McGuffey, Mindy Farmer, Brian Campbell, Stevie Van Gordon, Sherry Gaston, Katrina Reed, Elizabeth Wilkins, JJ Snidow, and Jim Williamson. They made the book better by exposing me to new ideas and experiences.

I've been fortunate to have Darrell Stark, Nate Ellis, Bill Zaboski, Craig Baldwin, Jamil Jivani, Ethan (Doug) Fallang, Kyle Walsh, and Aaron Kash in my life, and I consider each of them more brother than friend. I've been fortunate, too, to have mentors and friends of incredible ability, each of whom ensured that I had access to opportunities I simply didn't deserve. They include: Ron Selby, Mike Stratton, Shannon Arledge, Shawn Haney, Brad Nelson, David Frum, Matt Johnson, Judge David

Bunning, Reihan Salam, Ajay Royan, Fred Moll, and Peter Thiel. Many of these folks read versions of the manuscript and provided critical feedback.

I owe an incredible amount to my family, especially those who opened their hearts and shared memories, no matter how difficult or painful. My sister Lindsay Ratliff and Aunt Wee (Lori Meibers) deserve special thanks, both for helping me write this book and for supporting me throughout my life. I'm also grateful to Jim Vance, Dan Meibers, Kevin Ratliff, Mom, Bonnie Rose Meibers, Hannah Meibers, Kameron Ratliff, Meghan Ratliff, Emma Ratliff, Hattie Hounshell Blanton, Don Bowman (my dad), Cheryl Bowman, Cory Bowman, Chelsea Bowman, Lakshmi Chilukuri, Krish Chilukuri, Shreya Chilukuri, Donna Vance, Rachael Vance, Nate Vance, Lilly Hudson Vance, Daisy Hudson Vance, Gail Huber, Allan Huber, Mike Huber, Nick Huber, Denise Blanton, Arch Stacy, Rose Stacy, Rick Stacy, Amber Stacy, Adam Stacy, Taheton Stacy, Betty Sebastian, David Blanton, Gary Blanton, Wanda Blanton, Pet Blanton, Teaberry Blanton, and every crazy hillbilly I've ever had the honor to call my kin.

Last, but certainly not least, is my darling wife, Usha, who read every single word of my manuscript literally dozens of times, offered needed feedback (even when I didn't want it!), supported me when I felt like quitting, and celebrated with me during times of progress. So much of the credit for both this book and the happy life I lead belongs to her. Though it is one of the great regrets of my life that Mamaw and Papaw never met her, it is the source of my greatest joy that I did.

Notes

_____

1. Razib Khan, "The Scots-Irish as Indigenous People," *Discover* (July 22, 2012), http://blogs.discovermagazine.com/gnxp/2012/07/the-scots-irish-as-indigenous-people/#.VY8zEBNViko.

2. "Kentucky Feudist Is Killed," *The New York Times* (November 3, 1909).

3. Ibid.

4. Phillip J. Obermiller, Thomas E. Wagner, and E. Bruce Tucker, *Appalachian Odyssey: Historical Perspectives on the Great Migration,* (Westport, CT: Praeger, 2000), Chapter 1.

5. Ibid.; Khan, "The Scots-Irish as Indigenous People."

6. Jack Temple Kirby, "The Southern Exodus, 1910–1960: A Primer for Historians," *The Journal of Southern History* 49, no. 4 (November 1983), 585–600.

7. Ibid.

8. Ibid., 598.

9. Carl E. Feather, *Mountain People in a Flat Land: A Popular History of Appalachian Migration to Northeast Ohio, 1940–1965* (Athens: Ohio University Press, 1998), 4.

10. Obermiller, *Appalachian Odyssey*, 145.

11. Kirby, "The Southern Exodus," 598.

12. Elizabeth Kneebone, Carey Nadeau, and Alan Berube, "The Re-Emergence of Concentrated Poverty: Metropolitan Trends in the 2000s," Brookings Institution (November 2011), http://www.brookings.edu/research/papers/2011/11/03-poverty-kneebone-nadeau-berube.

13. "Nice Work if You Can Get Out," *The Economist* (April 2014), http://www.economist.com/news/finance-and-economics/21600989-why-rich-now-have-less-leisure-poor-nice-work-if-you-can-get-out.

14. Robert P. Jones and Daniel Cox, "Beyond Guns and God." Public Religion Institute (2012), http://publicreligion.org/site/wp-content/uploads/2012/09/WWC-Report-For-Web-Final.pdf.

15. *American Hollow* (documentary), directed by Rory Kennedy (USA, 1999).

16. Linda Gorman, "Is Religion Good for You?," The National Bureau of Economic Research, http://www.nber.org/digest/oct05/w11377.html.

17. Raj Chetty, et al., "Equality of Opportunity Project." Equality of Opportunity." 2014. http://www.equality-of-opportunity.org. (The authors' "Rel. Tot. variable" measures religiosity in a given region. The South and Rust Belt score much lower than many regions of the country.)

18. Ibid.

19. Carol Howard Merritt, "Why Evangelicalism Is Failing a New Generation," The Huffington Post: Religion (May 2010), http://www.huffingtonpost.com/carol-howard-merritt/why-evangelicalism-is-fai_b_503971.html.

20. Rick Perlstein, *Nixonland: The Rise of a President and the Fracturing of America* (New York: Scribner, 2008).

21. "Only 6% Rate News Media as Very Trustworthy," Rasmussen Report. February 28, 2013, http://www.rasmussenreports.com/public_content/politics/general_politics/february_2013/only_6_rate_news_media_as_very_trustworthy (accessed November 17, 2015).